To the Holy Shrines

Alexandria, 1853

SIR RICHARD BURTON
To the Holy Shrines

GREAT

JOURNEYS

TED SMART

PENGUIN BOOKS

Published by the Penguin Group
Penguin Books Ltd, 80 Strand, London WC2R ORL, England
Penguin Group (USA) Inc., 375 Hudson Street, New York, New York 10014, USA
Penguin Group (Canada), 90 Eglinton Avenue East, Suite 700, Toronto, Ontario, Canada M4P 2Y3
(a division of Pearson Penguin Canada Inc.)
Penguin Ireland, 25 St Stephen's Green, Dublin 2, Ireland (a division of Penguin Books Ltd)
Penguin Group (Australia), 250 Camberwell Road, Camberwell, Victoria 3124, Australia
(a division of Pearson Australia Group Pty Ltd)
Penguin Books India Pvt Ltd, 11 Community Centre, Panchsheel Park, New Delhi – 110 017, India
Penguin Group (NZ), 67 Apollo Drive, Rosedale, North Shore 0632, New Zealand
(a division of Pearson New Zealand Ltd)
Penguin Books (South Africa) (Pty) Ltd, 24 Sturdee Avenue, Rosebank, Johannesburg 2196, South Africa

Penguin Books Ltd, Registered Offices: 80 Strand, London WC2R ORL, England

www.penguin.com

Personal Narrative of a Pilgrimage to Al-Madinah and Meccah first published 1855
This extract published in Penguin Books 2007

3

All rights reserved

Inside-cover maps by Jeff Edwards

Typeset by Rowland Phototypesetting Ltd, Bury St Edmunds, Suffolk
Printed in England by Clays Ltd, St Ives plc

ISBN: 978-0-141-02538-4

This edition produced for The Book People Ltd,
Hall Wood Avenue, Haydock, St. Helens, WA11 9UL

Contents

In a crowded field, Sir Richard Burton (1821–90) may have a fair claim to be the most enjoyable of all Victorians: explorer, spy, linguist, sexologist, translator and a writer of overwhelming talent, Burton spent much of his life wandering the world and writing about it.

This sample from his great early work *Personal Narrative of a Pilgrimage to Al-Madinah and Meccah* tells the scarcely credible story of how in 1853 Burton successfully disguised himself as a Persian dervish and travelled from Egypt to Medina and Mecca, cities barred to all non-Moslems. These extracts describe his time in Egypt, the memorable crossing of the Red Sea to Yambu' and the journey through the Hijaz to Medina, giving a vivid sense of Burton's love of the Arab world. Spellings in the text have not been modernized. Burton is the master of the garrulous footnote and as many of these have been kept as possible: some are so long, however, that it has been necessary to convert them all into endnotes.

To Alexandria

On the evening of April 3, 1853, I left London for Southampton. By the advice of a brother officer, Captain (now Colonel) Henry Grindlay, of the Bengal Cavalry, – little thought at that time the adviser or the advised how valuable was the suggestion! – my Eastern dress was called into requisition before leaving town, and all my 'impedimenta' were taught to look exceedingly Oriental. Early the next day a 'Persian Prince,' accompanied by Captain Grindlay, embarked on board the Peninsular and Oriental Company's magnificent screw steamer 'Bengal.'

A fortnight was profitably spent in getting into the train of Oriental manners. For what polite Chesterfield says of the difference between a gentleman and his reverse, – namely, that both perform the same offices of life, but each in a several and widely different way – is notably as applicable to the manners of the Eastern as of the Western man. Look, for instance, at that Indian Moslem drinking a glass of water. With us the operation is simple enough, but his performance includes no fewer than five novelties. In the first place he clutches his tumbler as though it were the throat of a foe; secondly, he ejaculates, 'In the name of Allah the Compassionate, the Merciful!' before wetting his lips; thirdly, he imbibes the contents, swallowing them, not sipping them as he ought to do, and ending with a satisfied grunt; fourthly, before setting down the cup, he sighs forth, 'Praise be to Allah!' – of which you will understand the full meaning in the Desert; and, fifthly, he replies, 'May Allah make it pleasant to thee!' in answer to his friend's polite 'Pleasurably and health!' Also he is careful to avoid the irreligious action of drinking the pure element in a standing position, mindful, however, of the three recognised exceptions, the fluid of the Holy Well Zemzem, water distributed in charity, and that which remains after Wuzu, the lesser ablution. Moreover, in Europe, where both extremities are used indiscriminately, one forgets the exclusive use of the right hand, the manipulation of the rosary, the abuse of the chair, – your genuine Oriental gathers up his legs, looking almost as comfortable in it as a sailor upon the back of a high-trotting horse – the rolling gait with the toes straight to the front, the grave look and the habit of pious ejaculations.

Our voyage over the 'summer sea' was eventless. In a steamer of two or three thousand tons you discover the once dreaded, now contemptible, 'stormy waters' only by the band – a standing nuisance be it remarked – performing

> 'There we lay
> All the day,
> In the Bay of Biscay, O!'

The sight of glorious Trafalgar[1] excites none of the sentiments with which a tedious sail used to invest it.

'Gib' is, probably, better known to you, by Théophile Gautier and Eliot Warburton, than the regions about Cornhill; besides which, you anchor under the Rock exactly long enough to land and to breakfast. Malta, too, wears an old familiar face, which bids you order a dinner and superintend the iceing of claret (beginning of Oriental barbarism), instead of galloping about on donkey-back through fiery air in memory of St Paul and White-Cross Knights. But though our journey might be called monotonous, there was nothing to complain of. The ship was in every way comfortable; the cook, strange to say, was good, and the voyage lasted long enough, and not too long. On the evening of the thirteenth day after our start, the big-trowsered pilot, so lovely in his deformities to western eyes, made his appearance, and the good screw 'Bengal' found herself at anchor off the Headland of Clay.

Having been invited to start from the house of a kind friend, John W. Larking, I disembarked with him, and rejoiced to see that by dint of a beard and a shaven head I had succeeded, like the Lord of Geesh, in 'misleading the inquisitive spirit of the populace.' The mingled herd of spectators before whom we passed in review on the landing-place, hearing an audible 'Alhamdolillah'² whispered 'Muslim!' The infant population spared me the compliments usually addressed to hatted heads; and when a little boy, presuming that the occasion might possibly open the hand of generosity, looked in my face and exclaimed 'Bakhshísh,' he obtained in reply a 'Mafísh;' which convinced the bystanders that the sheep-skin covered a real sheep. We then mounted a

3

carriage, fought our way through the donkeys, and in half an hour found ourselves, chibúk in mouth and coffee-cup in hand, seated on the díwán of my friend Larking's hospitable home.

Wonderful was the contrast between the steamer and that villa on the Mahmudiyah canal! Startling the sudden change from presto to adagio life! In thirteen days we had passed from the clammy grey fog, that atmosphere of industry which kept us at anchor off the Isle of Wight, through the loveliest air of the Inland Sea, whose sparkling blue and purple haze spread charms even on N. Africa's beldame features, and now we are sitting silent and still, listening to the monotonous melody of the East – the soft night-breeze wandering through starlit skies and tufted trees, with a voice of melancholy meaning.

And this is the Arab's *Kayf.* The savouring of animal existence; the passive enjoyment of mere sense; the pleasant languor, the dreamy tranquillity, the airy castle-building, which in Asia stand in lieu of the vigorous, intensive, passionate life of Europe. It is the result of a lively, impressible, excitable nature, and exquisite sensibility of nerve; it argues a facility for voluptuousness unknown to northern regions, where happiness is placed in the exertion of mental and physical powers; where *Ernst ist das Leben;* where niggard earth commands ceaseless sweat of face, and damp chill air demands perpetual excitement, exercise, or change, or adventure, or dissipation, for want of something better. In the East, man wants but rest and shade: upon the banks of a bubbling stream, or under the cool shelter

4

of a perfumed tree, he is perfectly happy, smoking a pipe, or sipping a cup of coffee, or drinking a glass of sherbet, but above all things deranging body and mind as little as possible; the trouble of conversations, the displeasures of memory, and the vanity of thought being the most unpleasant interruptions to his *Kayf*. No wonder that 'Kayf' is a word untranslatable in our mother-tongue![3]

Let others describe the once famous Capital of Egypt, this City of Misnomers, whose dry docks are ever wet, and whose marble fountain is eternally dry, whose 'Cleopatra's Needle' is neither a needle nor Cleopatra's; whose 'Pompey's Pillar' never had any earthly connection with Pompey; and whose Cleopatra's Baths are, according to veracious travellers, no baths at all. Yet it is a wonderful place, this 'Libyan suburb' of our day, this outpost of civilisation planted upon the skirts of barbarism, this Osiris seated side by side with Typhon, his great old enemy. Still may be said of it, 'it ever beareth something new;' and Alexandria, a threadbare subject in Bruce's time, is even yet, from its perpetual changes, a fit field for modern description.

The better to blind the inquisitive eyes of servants and visitors, my friend, Larking, lodged me in an outhouse, where I could revel in the utmost freedom of life and manners. And although some Armenian Dragoman, a restless spy like all his race, occasionally remarked *voilà un Persan diablement dégagé*, none, except those who were entrusted with the secret, had any idea of the part I was playing. The domestics, devout Moslems, pronounced me an 'Ajami,[4] a kind of

Mohammedan, not a good one like themselves, but, still better than nothing. I lost no time in securing the assistance of a Shaykh,[5] and plunged once more into the intricacies of the Faith; revived my recollections of religious ablutions, read the Koran, and again became an adept in the art of prostration. My leisure hours were employed in visiting the baths and coffee-houses, in attending the bazars, and in shopping, – an operation which hereabouts consists of sitting upon a chapman's counter, smoking, sipping coffee, and telling your beads the while, to show that you are not of the slaves for whom time is made; in fact, in pitting your patience against that of your adversary, the vendor. I found time for a short excursion to a country village on the banks of the canal; nor was an opportunity of seeing 'Al-nahl,' the 'Bee-dance,' neglected, for it would be some months before my eyes might dwell on such a pleasant spectacle again.

Careful of graver matters, I attended the mosque, and visited the venerable localities in which modern Alexandria abounds. Pilgrimaging Moslems are here shown the tomb of Al-nabi Daniyal (Daniel the Prophet), discovered upon a spot where the late Sultan Mahmúd dreamed that he saw an ancient man at prayer. Sikandar al-Rumi, the Moslem Alexander the Great, of course left his bones in the place bearing his name, or, as he ought to have done so, bones have been found for him. Alexandria also boasts of two celebrated Walís – holy men. One is Mohammed al-Busiri, the author of a poem called Al-Burdah, universally read by the world of Islam, and locally recited at funerals and on other solemn occasions. The other is Abu Abbas al-Andalúsi, a sage and saint of the first water, at whose tomb prayer is never breathed in vain.

It is not to be supposed that the people of Alexandria could look upon my phials and pill-boxes without a yearning for their contents. An Indian doctor, too, was a novelty to them; Franks they despised, – but a man who had come so far from East and West! Then there was something infinitely seducing in the character of a magician, doctor, and fakír, each admirable of itself, thus combined to make 'great medicine.' Men, women, and children besieged my door, by which means I could see the people face to face, and especially the fair sex, of which Europeans, generally speaking, know only the worst specimens. Even respectable natives, after witnessing a performance of 'Mandal' and the Magic mirror,[6] opined that the stranger was a holy man, gifted with supernatural powers, and knowing everything. One old person sent to offer me his daughter in marriage; he said nothing about dowry, – but I thought proper to decline the honour. And a middle-aged lady proffered me the sum of one hundred piastres, nearly one pound sterling, if I would stay at Alexandria, and superintend the restoration of her blind left eye.

But the reader must not be led to suppose that I acted 'Carabin' or 'Sangrado' without any knowledge of my trade. From youth I have always been a dabbler in medical and mystical study. Moreover, the practice of physic is comparatively easy amongst dwellers in warm latitudes, uncivilised peoples, where there is not that complication of maladies which troubles more polished nations. And further, what simplifies extremely the treatment of the sick in these parts is the undoubted periodicity of disease, reducing almost all to one type – ague. Many of the complaints of tropical climates, as medical men well know, display palpably intermittent symptoms little known to colder countries; and speaking from individual experience, I may safely assert that in all cases of suffering, from a wound to ophthalmia, this phenomenon has forced itself upon my notice. So much by way of excuse. I therefore considered myself as well qualified for the work as if I had taken out a *buono per l'estero* diploma at Padua, and not more likely to do active harm than most of the regularly graduated young surgeons who start to 'finish' themselves upon the frame of the British soldier.

After a month's hard work at Alexandria, I prepared to assume the character of a wandering Darwaysh; after reforming my title from 'Mirza'[7] to 'Shaykh' Abdullah.[8] A reverend man, whose name I do not care to quote, some time ago initiated me into his order, the Kadiriyah, under the high-sounding name of Bismillah-Shah:[9] and, after a due period of probation, he graciously elevated me to the proud position of a Murshid,[10] or Master in the mystic craft. I was therefore sufficiently well acquainted with the tenets and practices of these Oriental Freemasons. No character in the Moslem world is so proper for disguise as that of the Darwaysh. It is assumed by all ranks, ages, and creeds; by the nobleman who has been disgraced at court, and by the peasant who is too idle to till the ground; by Dives, who is weary of life, and by Lazarus, who begs his bread from door to door. Further, the Darwaysh is allowed to ignore ceremony and politeness, as one who ceases to appear upon the stage of life; he may pray or not, marry or remain single as he pleases, be respectable in cloth of frieze as in cloth of gold, and no one asks him – the chartered vagabond – Why he comes here? or Wherefore he goes there? He may wend his way on foot alone, or ride his Arab mare followed by a dozen servants; he is equally feared without weapons, as swaggering through the streets armed to the teeth. The more haughty and offensive he is to the people, the more they respect him; a decided advantage to the traveller of choleric temperament. In the hour of imminent danger, he has only to become a maniac, and he is safe; a madman in the East, like a notably eccentric character in the West, is allowed to say or do whatever the spirit directs. Add to this character a little knowledge of medicine, a 'moderate skill in magic, and a reputation for caring for nothing but study and books,' together with capital sufficient to save you from the chance of starving, and you appear in the East to peculiar advantage. The only danger of the 'Mystic Path'[11] is, that the Darwaysh's ragged coat not unfrequently covers the cut-throat, and, if seized in the society of such a 'brother,' you may reluctantly become his companion, under the stick or on the stake.

[. . .]

Restlessness

The thorough-bred wanderer's idiosyncracy I presume to be a composition of what phrenologists call 'in-habitiveness' and 'locality' equally and largely developed. After a long and toilsome march, weary of the way, he drops into the nearest place of rest to become the most domestic of men. For a while he smokes the 'pipe of permanence'[1] with an infinite zest; he delights in vari-ous siestas during the day, relishing withal deep sleep during the dark hours; he enjoys dining at a fixed dinner hour, and he wonders at the demoralisation of the mind which cannot find means of excitement in chit-chat or small talk, in a novel or a newspaper. But soon the passive fit has passed away; again a paroxysm of ennui coming on by slow degrees, Viator loses appe-tite, he walks about his room all night, he yawns at conversations, and a book acts upon him as a narcotic. The man wants to wander, and he must do so, or he shall die.

After about a month most pleasantly spent at Alexandria, I perceived the approach of the enemy, and as nothing hampered my incomings and outgoings, I surrendered. The world was 'all before me,' and there was pleasant excitement in plunging single-handed into its chilling depths.

Planning for the Journey

Then I had to provide myself with certain necessaries for the way. These were not numerous. The silver-mounted dressing-bag is here supplied by a rag containing a Miswák[1] or tooth-stick, a bit of soap and a comb, wooden, for bone and tortoiseshell are not, religiously speaking, correct. Equally simple was my wardrobe; a change or two of clothing. It is a great mistake to carry too few clothes, and those who travel as Orientals should always have at least one very grand suit for use on critical occasions. Throughout the East a badly dressed man is a pauper, and, as in England, a pauper – unless he belongs to an order having a right to be poor – is a scoundrel. The only article of canteen description was a Zemzemiyah, a goat-skin water-bag, which, especially when new, communicates to its contents a ferruginous aspect and a wholesome, though hardly an attractive, flavour of tanno-gelatine. This was a necessary; to drink out of a tumbler, possibly fresh from pig-eating lips, would have entailed a certain loss of reputation. For bedding and furniture I had a coarse Persian rug – which, besides being couch, acted as chair, table, and oratory – a cotton-stuffed chintz-covered pillow, a blanket in case of cold, and a sheet, which did duty for tent and mosquito curtains in nights of heat.[2] As shade is a convenience not always procurable, another necessary was a huge cotton umbrella of Eastern make, brightly yellow, suggesting the idea of an overgrown marigold. I had also a substantial housewife, the gift of a kind relative, Miss Elizabeth Stisted; it was a roll of canvas, carefully soiled, and garnished with needles and thread, cobblers' wax, buttons, and other such articles. These things were most useful in lands where tailors abound not; besides which, the sight of a man darning his coat or patching his slippers teems with pleasing ideas of humility. A dagger,[3] a brass inkstand and pen-holder stuck in the belt, and a mighty rosary, which on occasion might have been converted into a weapon of offence, completed my equipment. I must not omit to mention the proper method of carrying money, which in these lands should never be entrusted to box or bag. A common cotton purse secured in a breast pocket (for Egypt now abounds in that civilised animal, the pick-pocket),[4] contained silver pieces and small change.[5] My gold, of which I carried twenty-five sovereigns, and papers, were committed to a substantial leathern belt of Maghrabi manufacture, made to be strapped round the waist under the dress. This is the Asiatic method of concealing valuables, and one more civilised than ours in the last century, when Roderic Random and his companion 'sewed their money between the lining and the waistband of their breeches, except some loose silver for immediate expense on the road.' The great inconvenience of the belt is its weight, especially where dollars must be carried, as in Arabia, causing chafes and discomfort at night. Moreover, it can scarcely be called safe. In dangerous countries wary travellers will adopt surer precautions.[6]

A pair of common native Khurjín, or saddle-bags, contained my wardrobe; the bed was readily rolled up into a bundle; and for a medicine chest I bought a peagreen box with red and yellow flowers, capable of standing falls from a camel twice a day.

On the Nile Steamboat the 'Little Asthmatic'

To me there was double dulness in the scenery: it seemed to be Sind over again – the same morning mist and noon-tide glare; the same hot wind and heat clouds, and fiery sunset, and evening glow; the same pillars of dust and 'devils' of sand sweeping like giants over the plain; the same turbid waters of a broad, shallow stream studded with sand-banks and silt-isles, with crashing earth slips and ruins nodding over a kind of cliff, whose base the stream gnaws with noisy tooth. On the banks, saline ground sparkled and glittered like hoar-frost in the sun; and here and there mud villages, solitary huts, pigeon-towers, or watch turrets, whence little brown boys shouted and slung stones at the birds, peeped out from among bright green patches of palm-tree, tamarisk, and mimosa, of maize, tobacco, and sugar-cane. Beyond the narrow tongue of land on the river banks lay the glaring, yellow Desert, with its low hills and sand slopes, bounded by innumerable pyramids of Nature's architecture. The boats, with their sharp bows, preposterous sterns, and lateen sails, might have belonged to the Indus. So might the chocolate-skinned, blue-robed peasantry; the women carrying progeny on their hips, with the eternal waterpot on their heads; and the men sleeping in the shade or following the plough, to which probably

Osiris first put hand. The lower animals, like the higher, were the same; gaunt, mange-stained camels, muddy buffaloes, scurvied donkeys, sneaking jackals, and fox-like dogs. Even the feathered creatures were perfectly familiar to my eye – paddy birds, pelicans, giant cranes, kites and wild waterfowl.

I had taken a third-class or deck-passage, whereby the evils of the journey were exasperated. A roasting sun pierced the canvas awning like hot water through a gauze veil, and by night the cold dews fell raw and thick as a Scotch mist. The cooking was abominable, and the dignity of Darwaysh-hood did not allow me to sit at meat with Infidels or to eat the food which they had polluted. So the Pilgrim squatted apart, smoking perpetually, with occasional interruptions to say his prayers and to tell his beads upon the mighty rosary; and he drank the muddy water of the canal out of a leathern bucket, and he munched his bread and garlic[1] with a desperate sanctimoniousness.

The 'Little Asthmatic' was densely crowded, and discipline not daring to mark out particular places, the scene on board of her was motley enough. There were two Indian officers, who naturally spoke to none but each other, drank bad tea, and smoked their cigars exclusively like Britons. A troop of the Kurd Kawwas,[2] escorting treasure, was surrounded by a group of noisy Greeks; these men's gross practical jokes sounding anything but pleasant to the solemn Moslems, whose saddle-bags and furniture were at every moment in danger of being defiled by abominable drinks and the ejected juices of tobacco. There was one pretty woman on board, a Spanish girl, who looked strangely mis-placed – a rose in a field of thistles. Some silent Italians, with noisy interpreters, sat staidly upon the benches. It was soon found out, through the communicative dragoman, that their business was to buy horses for H. M. of Sardinia: they were exposed to a volley of questions delivered by a party of French tradesmen returning to Cairo, but they shielded themselves and fought shy with Machiavellian dexterity. Besides these was a German, a 'beer-bottle in the morning and a bottle of beer in the evening,' to borrow a simile from his own nation; a Syrian merchant, the richest and ugliest of Alexandria; and a few French house-painters going to decorate the Pasha's palace at Shubrá.

Life in the Wakálah

The 'Wakálah,' as the Caravanserai or Khán is called in Egypt, combines the offices of hotel, lodging-house, and store. It is at Cairo, as at Constantinople, a massive pile of buildings surrounding a quadrangular 'Hosh' or court-yard. On the ground-floor are rooms like caverns for merchandise, and shops of different kinds – tailors, cobblers, bakers, tobacconists, fruiterers, and others. A roofless gallery or a covered verandah, into which all the apartments open, runs round the first and some-times the second story: the latter, however, is usually exposed to the sun and wind. The accommodations consist of sets of two or three rooms, generally an inner one and an outer; the latter contains a hearth for cooking, a bathing-place, and similar necessaries. The staircases are high, narrow, and exceedingly dirty; dark at night, and often in bad repair; a goat or donkey is tethered upon the different landings; here and there a fresh skin is stretched in process of tanning, and the smell reminds the veteran traveller of those closets in the old French inns where cat used to be prepared for playing the part of jugged hare. The interior is unfurnished; even the pegs upon which clothes are hung have been pulled down for fire-wood: the walls are bare but for stains, thick cobwebs depend in fes-toons from the blackened rafters of the ceiling, and the stone floor would disgrace a civilised prison: the windows are huge apertures carefully barred with wood or iron, and in rare places show remains of glass or paper pasted over the framework. In the courtyard the poorer sort of travellers consort with tethered beasts of burden, beggars howl, and slaves lie basking and scratching themselves upon mountainous heaps of cotton bales and other merchandise.

This is not a tempting picture, yet is the Wakalah a most amusing place, presenting a succession of scenes which would delight lovers of the Dutch school – a rich exemplification of the grotesque, and what is called by artists the 'dirty picturesque.'

I could find no room in the Wakalah Khan Khalíl, the Long's, or Meurice's of native Cairo; I was therefore obliged to put up with the Jamáliyah, a Greek quarter, swarming with drunken Christians, and therefore about as fashionable as Oxford Street or Covent Garden. Even for this I had to wait a week. The pilgrims were flocking to Cairo, and to none other would the prudent hotel keepers open their doors, for the following sufficient reasons. When you enter a Wakalah, the first thing you have to do is to pay a small sum, varying from two to five shillings, for the Miftáh (the key). This is generally equivalent to a month's rent; so the sooner you leave the house the better for it. I was obliged to call myself a Turkish pilgrim in order to get possession of two most comfortless rooms, which I afterwards learned were celebrated for making travellers ill; and I had to pay eighteen piastres for the key and eighteen ditto per mensem for rent, besides five piastres to the man who swept and washed the place. So that for this month my house-hire amounted to nearly four pence a day.

But I was fortunate enough in choosing the Jamaliyah Wakalah, for I found a friend there. On board the steamer a fellow-voyager, seeing me sitting alone and therefore as he conceived in discomfort, placed himself by my side and opened a hot fire of kind inquiries. He was a man about forty-five, of middle size, with a large round head closely shaven, a bull-neck, limbs sturdy as a Saxon's, a thin red beard, and handsome features beaming with benevolence. A curious dry humour he had, delighting in 'quizzing,' but in so quiet, solemn, and quaint a way that before you knew him you could scarcely divine his drift.

'Thank Allah, we carry a doctor!' said my friend more than once, with apparent fervour of gratitude, after he had discovered my profession. I was fairly taken in by the pious ejaculation, and some days elapsed before the drift of his remark became apparent.

'You doctors,' he explained, when we were more intimate, 'what do you do? A man goes to you for ophthalmia: it is a purge, a blister, and a drop in the eye! Is it for fever? well! a purge and kinákíná (quinine). For dysentery? a purge and extract of opium. Wa'llahi! I am as good a physician as the best of you,' he would add with a broad grin, 'if I only knew the Dirham-birhams, – drams and drachms, – and a few break-jaw Arabic names of diseases.'

Haji Wali[1] therefore emphatically advised me to make bread by honestly teaching languages. 'We are

19

doctor-ridden,' said he, and I found it was the case.

When we lived under the same roof, the Haji and I became fast friends. During the day we called on each other frequently, we dined together, and passed the evening in a Mosque, or some other place of public pastime. Coyly at first, but less guardedly as we grew bolder, we smoked the forbidden weed 'Hashish,[2]' conversing lengthily the while about that world of which I had seen so much. Originally from Russia, he also had been a traveller, and in his wanderings he had cast off most of the prejudices of his people. 'I believe in Allah and his Prophet, and in nothing else,' was his sturdy creed; he rejected alchemy, jinnis and magicians, and truly he had a most unoriental distaste for tales of wonder. When I entered the Wakalah, he constituted himself my cicerone, and especially guarded me against the cheating of tradesmen. By his advice I laid aside the Darwaysh's gown, the large blue pantaloons, and the short shirt; in fact all connection with Persia and the Persians. 'If you persist in being an 'Ajami,' said the Haji, 'you will get yourself into trouble; in Egypt you will be cursed; in Arabia you will be beaten because you are a heretic; you will pay the treble of what other travellers do, and if you fall sick you may die by the roadside.' After long deliberation about the choice of nations, I became a 'Pathán.[3]' Born in India of Afghan parents, who had settled in the country, educated at Rangoon, and sent out to wander, as men of that race frequently are, from early youth, I was well guarded against the danger of detection by a fellow-countryman. To support the character requires a knowledge of Persian, Hindustani and Arabic, all of which I knew sufficiently well to pass muster; any trifling inaccuracy was charged upon my long residence at Rangoon. This was an important step; the first question at the shop, on the camel, and in the Mosque, is 'What is thy name?' the second, 'Whence comest thou?' This is not generally impertinent, or intended to be annoying; if, however, you see any evil intention in the questioner, you may rather roughly ask him, 'What may be his maternal parent's name?' – equivalent to enquiring, *Anglicè*, in what church his mother was married, – and escape your difficulties under cover of the storm. But this is rarely necessary. I assumed the polite, pliant manners of an Indian physician, and the dress of a small Effendi (or gentleman), still, however, representing myself to be a Darwaysh, and frequenting the places where Darwayshes congregate. 'What business,' asked the Haji, 'have those reverend men with politics or statistics, or any of the information which you are collecting? Call yourself a religious wanderer if you like, and let those who ask the object of your peregrinations know that you are under a vow to visit all the holy places in Al-Islam. Thus you will persuade them that you are a man of rank under a cloud, and you will receive much more civility than perhaps you deserve,' concluded my friend with a dry laugh. The remark proved his sagacity; and after ample experience I had not to repent having been guided by his advice.

The Cost of Living in Cairo

Perhaps the reader may be curious to see the necessary expenses of a bachelor residing at Cairo. He must observe, however, in the following list that I was not a strict economist, and, besides that, I was a stranger in the country: inhabitants and old settlers would live as well for little more than two-thirds the sum.

		Piastres.	Faddah.
House rent at 18 piastres per mensem		0	24
Servant at 80 piastres per do.		2	26
Breakfast for self and servant.	10 eggs	0	5
	Coffee	0	10
	Water melon (now 5 piastres)	1	0
	Two rolls of bread	0	10
Dinner.	2 lbs. of meat	2	20
	Two rolls of bread	0	10
	Vegetables	0	20
	Rice	0	5
	Oil and clarified butter	1	0
Sundries.	A skin of Nile water	1	0
	Tobacco[1]	1	0
	Hammám (hot bath)	3	20
	Total	12	50

Equal to about two shillings and sixpence.

The Ramazan

Like the Italian, the Anglo-Catholic, and the Greek fasts, the chief effect of the 'blessed month' upon True Believers is to darken their tempers into positive gloom. Their voices, never of the softest, acquire, especially after noon, a terribly harsh and creaking tone. The men curse one another[1] and beat the women. The women slap and abuse the children, and these in their turn cruelly entreat, and use bad language to, the dogs and cats. You can scarcely spend ten minutes in any populous part of the city without hearing some violent dispute. The 'Karakún,' or station-houses, are filled with lords who have administered an undue dose of chastisement to their ladies, and with ladies who have scratched, bitten, and otherwise injured the bodies of their lords. The Mosques are crowded with a sulky, grumbling population, making themselves offensive to one another on earth whilst working their way to heaven; and in the shade, under the outer walls, the little boys who have been expelled the church attempt to forget their miseries in spiritless play. In the bazars and streets, pale long-drawn faces, looking for the most part intolerably cross, catch your eye, and at this season a stranger will sometimes meet with positive incivility. A shopkeeper, for instance, usually says when he rejects an insufficient offer, 'Yaftah Allah,' – 'Allah opens.[2]' During the Ramazan, he will grumble about the bore

23

of Ghashím, or 'Johnny raws,' and gruffly tell you not to stand there wasting his time. But as a rule the shops are either shut or destitute of shopmen, merchants will not purchase, and students will not study. In fine, the Ramazan, for many classes, is one-twelfth of the year wantonly thrown away.

The following is the routine of a fast day. About half an hour after midnight, the gun sounds its warning to faithful men that it is time to prepare for the 'Sahúr,' (early breakfast) or morning meal. My servant then wakes me, if I have slept; brings water for ablution, spreads the Sufrah (or leather cloth); and places before me certain remnants of the evening's meal. It is some time before the stomach becomes accustomed to such hours, but in matters of appetite, habit is everything, and for health's sake one should strive to eat as plentifully as possible. Then sounds the Salám, or Blessings on the Prophet, an introduction to the Call of Morning Prayer. Smoking sundry pipes with tenderness, as if taking leave of a friend; and until the second gun, fired at about half-past two A.M., gives the Imsák, – the order to abstain from food, – I wait the Azán,[3] which in this month is called somewhat earlier than usual. Then, after a ceremony termed the Níyat (purpose) of fasting, I say my prayers, and prepare for repose. At 7 A.M. the labours of the day begin for the working classes of society; the rich spend the night in revelling, and rest in down from dawn till noon.

The first thing on rising is to perform the Wuzu, or lesser ablution, which invariably follows sleep in a reclining position; without this it would be improper to pray, to enter the Mosques, to approach a religious man, or to touch the Koran. A few pauper patients usually visit me at this hour, report the phenomena of their complaints, – which they do, by the bye, with unpleasant minuteness of detail, – and receive fresh instructions. At 9 A.M. Shaykh Mohammed enters, with 'lecture' written upon his wrinkled brow; or I pick him up on the way, and proceed straight to the Mosque Al-Azhar. After three hours' hard reading, with little interruption from bystanders – this is long vacation, most of the students being at home – comes the call to mid-day prayer. The founder of Al-Islam ordained but few devotions for the morning, which is the business part of the Eastern day; but during the afternoon and evening they succeed one another rapidly, and their length increases. It is then time to visit my rich patients, and afterwards, by way of accustoming myself to the sun, to wander among the bookshops for an hour or two, or simply to idle in the street. At 3 P.M. I return home, recite the afternoon prayers, and re-apply myself to study.

This is the worst part of the day. In Egypt the summer nights and mornings are, generally speaking, pleasant, but the forenoons are sultry, and the afternoons are serious. A wind wafting the fine dust and furnace-heat of the desert blows over the city; the ground returns with interest the showers of caloric from above, and not a cloud or a vapour breaks the dreary expanse of splendour on high. There being no such comforts as Indian tatties, and few but the wealthiest houses boasting glass windows, the interior of your room is somewhat more fiery than the street. Weakened with fasting, the body feels the heat trebly, and the disordered stomach almost affects the brain. Every minute is counted with morbid fixity of idea as it passes on towards the blessed sunset, especially by those whose terrible lot is manual labour at such a season. A few try to forget their afternoon miseries in slumber, but most people take the Kaylúlah, or Siesta, shortly after the meridian, holding it unwholesome to sleep late in the day.

As the Maghrib, the sunset hour, approaches – and how slowly it comes! – the town seems to recover from a trance. People flock to the windows and balconies, in order to watch the moment of their release. Some pray, others tell their beads; while others, gathering together in groups or paying visits, exert themselves to while away the lagging time.

O Gladness! at length it sounds, that gun from the citadel. Simultaneously rises the sweet cry of the Mu'ezzin, calling men to prayer, and the second cannon booms from the Abbásíyah Palace, – 'Al Fitár! Al Fitar!' fast-breaking! fast-breaking! shout the people, and a hum of joy rises from the silent city. Your acute ears waste not a moment in conveying the delightful intelligence to your parched tongue, empty stomach, and languid limbs. You exhaust a pot full of water, no matter its size. You clap hurried hands[4] for a pipe; you order coffee; and provided with these comforts, you sit down, and calmly contemplate the coming pleasures of the evening.

Poor men eat heartily at once. The rich break their

fast with a light meal, – a little bread and fruit, fresh or dry, especially water-melon, sweetmeats, or such digestible dishes as 'Muhallabah,' – a thin jelly of milk, starch, and rice-flour. They then smoke a pipe, drink a cup of coffee or a glass of sherbet, and recite the evening prayers; for the devotions of this hour are delicate things, and while smoking a first pipe after sixteen hours' abstinence, time easily slips away. Then they sit down to the Fatúr (breakfast), *the* meal of the twenty-four hours, and eat plentifully, if they would avoid illness.

There are many ways of spending a Ramazan evening. The Egyptians have a proverb, like ours of the Salernitan school:

'After Al-Ghadá rest, if it be but for two moments: After Al-Ashá[5] walk, if it be but two steps.'

The streets are now crowded with a good-humoured throng of strollers; the many bent on pleasure, the few wending their way to the Mosque, where the Imam recites 'Taráwíh' prayers.[6] They saunter about, the accustomed pipe in hand, shopping, for the stalls are open till a late hour; or they sit in crowds at the coffee-house entrance, smoking Shíshas, (water-pipes), chatting, and listening to story-tellers, singers and itinerant preachers. Here a bare-footed girl trills and quavers, accompanied by a noisy tambourine and a 'scrannel pipe' of abominable discordance, in honour of a perverse saint whose corpse insisted upon being buried inside some respectable man's dwelling-house.[7] The scene reminds you strongly of the *Sonneurs* of Brittany and the *Zampognari* from the Abruzzian Highlands bagpiping before the Madonna. There a tall, gaunt Maghrabi displays upon a square yard of dirty paper certain lines and blots, supposed to represent the venerable Ka'abah, and collects coppers to defray the expenses of his pilgrimage. A steady stream of loungers sets through the principal thoroughfares towards the Azbakiyah Gardens, which skirt the Frank quarter; there they sit in the moonlight, listening to Greek and Turkish bands, or making merry with cakes, toasted grains, coffee, sugared-drinks, and the broad pleasantries of Kara Gyúz (the local Punch and Judy). Here the scene is less thoroughly Oriental than within the city; but the appearance of Frank dress amongst the varieties of Eastern costume, the moon-lit sky, and the light mist hanging over the deep shade of the Acacia trees – whose rich scented yellow-white blossoms are popularly compared to the old Pasha's beard – make it passing picturesque. And the traveller from the far East remarks with wonder the presence of certain ladies, whose only mark of modesty is the Burká, or face-veil: upon this laxity the police looks with lenient eyes, inasmuch as, until very lately, it paid a respectable tax to the state.

Returning to the Moslem quarter, you are bewildered by its variety of sounds. Everyone talks, and talking here is always in extremes, either in a whisper, or in a scream; gesticulation excites the lungs, and strangers cannot persuade themselves that men so converse without being or becoming furious. All the street cries, too, are in the soprano key. 'In thy protection! in thy protection!' shouts a Fellah peasant to a sentinel, who is flogging him towards the station-house, followed by a tail of women, screaming, 'Yá Gháratí – yá Dahwatí – yá Hasratí – yá Nidáma tí – O my calamity! O my shame!' The boys have elected a Pasha, whom they are conducting in procession, with wisps of straw for Mash'als, or cressets, and outrunners, all huzzaing with ten-schoolboy power. 'O thy right! O thy left! O thy face! O thy heel! O thy back, thy back!' cries the panting footman, who, huge torch on shoulder, runs before the grandee's carriage; 'Bless the Prophet and get out of the way!' 'O Allah bless him!' respond the good Moslems, some shrinking up to the walls to avoid the stick, others rushing across the road, so as to give themselves every chance of being knocked down. The donkey boy beats his ass with a heavy palm-cudgel, – he fears no treadmill here, – cursing him at the top of his voice for a 'pander,' a 'Jew,' a 'Christian,' and a 'son of the One-eyed, whose portion is Eternal Punishment.' 'O chick pease! O pips!' sings the vendor of parched grains, rattling the unsavoury load in his basket. 'Out of the way, and say, "There is one God,"' pants the industrious water-carrier, laden with a skin, fit burden for a buffalo. 'Sweet-water, and gladden thy soul, O lemonade!' pipes the seller of that luxury, clanging his brass cups together. Then come the beggars, intensely Oriental. 'My supper is in Allah's hands, my supper is in Allah's hands! whatever thou givest, that will go with thee!' chaunts the old vagrant, whose wallet perhaps contains more provision than the basket of many a respectable shopkeeper. 'Na'al abúk

– curse thy father – O brother of a naughty sister!' is the response of some petulant Greek to the touch of the old man's staff. 'The grave is darkness, and good deeds are its lamp!' sing the blind women, rapping two sticks together: 'upon Allah! upon Allah! O daughter!' cry the bystanders, when the obstinate 'bint'[8] (daughter) of sixty years seizes their hands, and will not let go without extorting a farthing. 'Bring the sweet' (i.e. fire), 'and take the full,' (i.e. empty cup), euphuistically cry the long-moustached, fierce-browed Arnauts to the coffee-house keeper, who stands by them charmed by the rhyming *repartee* that flows so readily from their lips.

'Han*ien*', may it be pleasant to thee! is the signal for encounter.

'Thou drinkest for *ten*,' replies the other, instead of returning the usual religious salutation.

'I am the cock and thou art the *hen!*' is the rejoinder, – a tart one.

'Nay, I am the thick one and thou art the *thin!*' resumes the first speaker, and so on till they come to equivoques which will not bear a literal English translation.

And sometimes, high above the hubbub, rises the melodious voice of the blind mu'ezzin, who, from his balcony in the beetling tower rings forth, 'Hie ye to devotion! Hie ye to salvation.' And (at morning-prayer time) he adds: 'Devotion is better than sleep! Devotion is better than sleep!' Then good Moslems piously stand up, and mutter, previous to prayer, 'Here am I at Thy call, O Allah! here am I at Thy call!'

Sometimes I walked with my friend to the citadel,

and sat upon a high wall, one of the outworks of Mohammed Ali's Mosque, enjoying a view which, seen by night, when the summer moon is near the full, has a charm no power of language can embody. Or escaping from 'stifled Cairo's filth,' we passed, through the Gate of Victory, into the wilderness beyond the City of the Dead. Seated upon some mound of ruins, we inhaled the fine air of the Desert, inspiriting as a cordial, when star-light and dew-mists diversified a scene, which, by day, is one broad sea of yellow loam with billows of chalk rock, thinly covered by a film-like spray of sand surging and floating in the fiery wind. There, within a mile of crowded life, all is desolate; the town walls seem crumbling to decay, the hovels are tenantless, and the paths untrodden; behind you lies the Wild, before you, the thousand tomb-stones, ghastly in their whiteness; while beyond them the tall dark forms of the Mamluk Soldans' towers rise from the low and hollow ground like the spirits of kings guarding ghostly subjects in the Shadowy Realm. Nor less weird than the scene are the sounds! – the hyæna's laugh, the howl of the wild dog, and the screech of the low-flying owl.

[…]

About half-an-hour before midnight sounds the Abrár or call to prayer, at which time the latest wanderers return home to prepare for the Sahur, their dawn meal. You are careful on the way to address each sentinel with a 'Peace be upon thee!' especially if you have no lantern, otherwise you may chance to sleep in the guardhouse. And, *chemin faisant*, you cannot but stop to gaze at streets as little like what civilised Europe understands by that name as is an Egyptian temple to the new Houses of Parliament.

There are certain scenes, cannily termed 'Kenspeckle,' which print themselves upon Memory, and which endure as long as Memory lasts, – a thunder-cloud bursting upon the Alps, a night of stormy darkness off the Cape, an African tornado, and, perhaps, most awful of all, a solitary journey over the sandy Desert.

Of this class is a stroll through the thoroughfares of old Cairo by night. All is squalor in the brilliancy of noon-day. In darkness you see nothing but a silhouette. When, however, the moon is high in the heavens, and the summer stars rain light upon God's world, there is something not of earth in the view. A glimpse at the strip of pale blue sky above scarcely reveals three ells of breadth: in many places the interval is less: here the copings meet, and there the outriggings of the houses seem to interlace. Now they are parted by a pencil of snowy sheen, then by a flood of silvery splendour; while under the projecting cornices and the huge hanging balcony-windows of fantastic wood-work, supported by gigantic brackets and corbels, and under deep verandahs, and gateways, vast enough for Behemoth to pass through, and in blind wynds and long cul-de-sacs, lie patches of thick darkness, made visible by the dimmest of oil lamps. The arch is a favourite feature: in one place you see it a mere skeleton-rib opening into some huge deserted hall; in another the ogre is full of fretted stone and wood carved like lace-work. Not a line is straight, the tall dead walls of the Mosques slope over their massy buttresses, and the thin minarets seem about to fall across your path. The cornices project crookedly from the houses, while the great gables stand merely by force of cohesion. And that the Line of Beauty may not be wanting, the graceful bending form of the palm, on whose topmost feathers, quivering in the cool night breeze, the moonbeam glistens, springs from a gloomy mound, or from the darkness of a mass of houses almost level with the ground. Briefly, the whole view is so strange, so fantastic, so ghostly, that it seems preposterous to imagine that in such places human beings like ourselves can be born, and live through life, and carry out the command 'increase and multiply,' and die.

The Albanian Captain

My departure from Cairo was hastened by an accident. I lost my reputation by a little misfortune that happened in this wise.

At Haji Wali's room in the Caravanserai, I met a Yuzbáshi, or captain of Albanian Irregulars, who was in Egypt on leave from Al-Hijaz. He was a tall, bony, and broad-shouldered mountaineer, about forty years old, with the large *bombé* brow, the fierce eyes, thin lips, lean jaws, and peaky chin of his race. His mustachios were enormously long and tapering, and the rest of his face, like his head, was close shaven. His *Fustan*[1] was none of the cleanest; nor was the red cap, which he wore rakishly pulled over his frowning forehead, quite free from stains. Not permitted to carry the favourite pistols, he contented himself with sticking his right hand in the empty belt, and stalking about the house with a most military mien. Yet he was as little of a bully as carpet knight, that same Ali Ághá; his body showed many a grisly scar, and one of his shin bones had been broken by a Turkish bullet, when he was playing tricks on the Albanian hills, – an accident inducing a limp, which he attempted to conceal by a heavy swagger. When he spoke, his voice was affectedly gruff; he had a sad knack of sneering, and I never saw him thoroughly sober.

34

Our acquaintance began with a kind of storm, which blew over, and left fine weather. I was showing Haji Wali my pistols with Damascene barrels when Ali Agha entered the room. He sat down before me with a grin, which said intelligibly enough, 'What business have *you* with weapons?' – snatched the arm out of my hand, and began to inspect it as a *connoisseur*. Not admiring this procedure, I wrenched it away from him, and, addressing myself to Haji Wali, proceeded quietly with my dissertation. The captain of Irregulars and I then looked at each other. He cocked his cap on one side, in token of excited pugnacity. I twirled my moustachios to display a kindred emotion. Had he been armed, and in Al-Hijaz, we should have fought it out at once, for the Arnauts are *'terribili colla pistola,'* as the Italians say, meaning that upon the least provocation they pull out a horse-pistol, and fire it in the face of friend or foe. Of course, the only way under these circumstances is to anticipate them; but even this desperate prevention seldom saves a stranger, as whenever there is danger, these men go about in pairs. I never met with a more reckless brood. Upon the line of march Albanian troops are not allowed ammunition; for otherwise there would be half a dozen duels a day. When they quarrel over their cups, it is the fashion for each man to draw a pistol, and to place it against his opponent's breast. The weapons being kept accurately clean, seldom miss fire, and if one combatant draw trigger before the other, he would immediately be shot down by the bystanders. In Egypt these men, – who are used as Irregulars, and are often quartered upon the hapless villagers, when unable or unwilling to pay taxes, – were the terror of the population. On many occasions they have quarrelled with foreigners, and insulted European women. In Al-Hijaz their recklessness awes even the Badawin. The townspeople say of them that, 'tripe-sellers, and bath-servants, at Stambul, they become Pharaohs (tyrants, ruffians,) in Arabia.' At Jeddah the Arnauts have amused themselves with firing at the English Consul, Mr Ogilvie, when he walked upon his terrace. And this man-shooting appears a favourite sport with them: at Cairo numerous stories illustrate the *sang froid* with which they used to knock over the camel-drivers, if any one dared to ride past their barracks. The Albanians vaunt their skill in using weapons, and their pretensions impose upon Arabs as well as Egyptians; yet I have never found them wonderful with any arm (the pistol alone excepted); and our officers, who have visited their native hills, speak of them as tolerable but by no means first-rate rifle shots.

The captain of Irregulars being unhappily debarred the pleasure of shooting me, after looking fierce for a time, rose, and walked majestically out of the room. A day or two afterwards, he called upon me civilly enough, sat down, drank a cup of coffee, smoked a pipe, and began to converse. But as he knew about a hundred Arabic words, and I as many Turkish, our conversation was carried on under difficulties. Presently he asked me in a whisper for ''Araki.'[2] I replied that there was none in the house, which induced a sneer and an ejaculation sounding like 'Himár,' (ass,) the slang synonym amongst fast Moslems for water-drinker. After rising to depart, he seized me waggishly, with an eye to a trial of strength. Thinking that an Indian doctor and a temperance man would not be very dangerous, he exposed himself to what is professionally termed a 'cross-buttock,' and had his 'nut' come in contact with the stone floor instead of my bed, he might not have drunk for many a day. The fall had a good effect upon his temper. He jumped up, patted my head, called for another pipe, and sat down to show me his wounds, and to boast of his exploits. I could not help remarking a ring of English gold, with a bezel of bloodstone, sitting strangely upon his coarse, sun-stained hand. He declared that it had been snatched by him from a Konsúl (Consul) at Jeddah, and he volubly related, in a mixture of Albanian, Turkish, and Arabic, the history of his acquisition. He begged me to supply him with a little poison that 'would not lie,' for the purpose of quieting a trouble-some enemy, and he carefully stowed away in his pouch five grains of calomel, which I gave him for that laud-able purpose. Before taking leave he pressed me strongly to go and drink with him; I refused to do so during the day, but, wishing to see how these men sacrifice to Bacchus, promised compliance that night. About nine o'clock, when the Caravanserai was quiet, I took a pipe, and a tobacco-pouch, stuck my dagger in my belt, and slipped into Ali Agha's room. He was sitting on a bed spread upon the ground: in front of him stood four wax candles (all Orientals hate drinking in any but a bright light), and a tray containing a basin of stuff like soup maigre, a dish of cold stewed meat, and two bowls of Salátah,[3] sliced cucumber, and curds. The 'materials' peeped out of an iron pot filled with water; one was a long, thin, white-glass flask of 'Araki, the other a bottle of some strong perfume. Both were wrapped up in wet rags, the usual refrigerator.

Ali Agha welcomed me politely, and seeing me admire the preparations, bade me beware how I suspected an Albanian of not knowing how to drink; he made me sit by him on the bed, threw his dagger to a handy distance, signalled me to do the same, and prepared to begin the bout. Taking up a little tumbler, in shape like those from which French postilions used to drink *la goutte*, he inspected it narrowly, wiped out the interior with his forefinger, filled it to the brim, and offered it to his guest[4] with a bow. I received it with a low salam, swallowed its contents at once, turned it upside down in proof of fair play, replaced it upon the floor, with a jaunty movement of the arm, somewhat like a pugilist delivering a 'rounder,' bowed again, and requested him to help himself. The same ceremony followed on his part. Immediately after each glass, – and rapidly the cup went about, – we swallowed a draught of water, and ate a spoonful of the meat or the Salatah in order to cool our palates. Then we re-applied ourselves to our pipes, emitting huge puffs, a sign of being 'fast' men, and looked facetiously at each other, – drinking being considered by Moslems a funny and pleasant sort of sin.

The Albanian captain was at least half seas over when we began the bout, yet he continued to fill and to drain without showing the least progress towards ebriety. I in vain for a time expected the *bad-masti* (as the Persians call it,) the horse play, and the gross facetiæ, which generally accompany southern and eastern tipsiness. Ali Agha, indeed, occasionally took up the bottle of perfume, filled the palm of his right hand, and dashed it in my face: I followed his example, but our pleasantries went no further.

Presently my companion started a grand project, namely, that I should entice the respectable Haji Wali into the room, where we might force him to drink. The idea was facetious; it was making a Bow-street magistrate polk at a casino. I started up to fetch the Haji; and when I returned with him Ali Agha was found in a new stage of 'freshness.' He had stuck a green-leaved twig upright in the floor, and had so turned over a gugglet of water, that its contents trickled slowly, in a tiny stream under the verdure; whilst he was sitting before it mentally gazing, with an outward show of grim Quixotic tenderness, upon the shady trees and the cool rills of his fatherland. Possibly he had peopled the place with 'young barbarians at play;' for verily I thought that a tear 'which had no business there' was glistening in his stony eye.

The appearance of Haji Wali suddenly changed the scene. Ali Agha jumped up, seized the visitor by the shoulder, compelled him to sit down, and, ecstasied by the old man's horror at the scene, filled a tumbler, and with the usual grotesque grimaces insisted upon its being drunk off. Haji Wali stoutly refused; then Ali Agha put it to his own lips, and drained it, with a hurt feeling and reproachful aspect. We made our unconvivial friend smoke a few puffs, and then we returned to the charge. In vain the Haji protested that throughout life he had avoided the deadly sin; in vain he promised to drink with us to-morrow, – in vain he quoted the Koran, and alternately coaxed, and threatened us with the police. We were inexorable. At last the Haji started upon his feet, and rushed away, regardless of any thing but escape, leaving his Tarbush, his slippers, and his pipe, in the hands of the enemy. The host did not dare to pursue his recreant guest beyond the door, but returning he carefully sprinkled the polluting liquid on the cap, pipe, and shoes, and called the Haji an ass in every tongue he knew.

Then we applied ourselves to supper, and dispatched the soup, the stew, and the Salatah. A few tumblers and pipes were exhausted to obviate indigestion, when Ali Agha arose majestically, and said that he required a troop of dancing girls to gladden his eyes with a ballet.

I represented that such persons are no longer admitted into Caravanserais.[5] He inquired, with calm ferocity, 'who hath forbidden it?' I replied 'the Pasha;' upon which Ali Agha quietly removed his cap, brushed it with his dexter fore-arm, fitted it on his forehead, raking forwards, twisted his mustachios to the sharp point of a single hair, shouldered his pipe, and moved towards the door, vowing that he would make the Pasha himself come, and dance before us.

I foresaw a brawl, and felt thankful that my boon companion had forgotten his dagger. Prudence whispered me to return to my room, to bolt the door, and to go to bed, but conscience suggested that it would be unfair to abandon the Albanian in his present helpless state. I followed him into the outer gallery, pulling him, and begging him, as a despairing wife might urge a drunken husband, to return home. And he, like the British husband, being greatly irritated by the unjovial advice, instantly belaboured with his pipe-stick the first person he met in the gallery, and sent him flying down the stairs with fearful shouts of 'O Egyptians! O ye accursed! O genus of Pharaoh! O race of dogs! O Egyptians!'

He then burst open a door with his shoulder, and reeled into a room where two aged dames were placidly reposing by the side of their spouses, who were basket-makers. They immediately awoke, seeing a stranger, and, hearing his foul words, they retorted with a hot volley of vituperation.

Put to flight by the old women's tongues, Ali Agha, in spite of all my endeavours, reeled down the stairs, and fell upon the sleeping form of the night porter, whose blood he vowed to drink – the Oriental form of threatening 'spiflication.' Happily for the assaulted, the Agha's servant, a sturdy Albanian lad, was lying on a mat in the doorway close by. Roused by the tumult, he jumped up, and found the captain in a state of fury. Apparently the man was used to the master's mood. Without delay he told us all to assist, and we lending a helping hand, half dragged and half carried the Albanian to his room. Yet even in this ignoble plight, he shouted with all the force of his lungs the old war-cry, 'O Egyptians! O race of dogs! I have dishonoured all Sikandariyah – all Kahirah – all Suways.⁶' And in this vaunting frame of mind he was put to bed. No Welsh undergraduate at Oxford, under similar circumstances, ever gave more trouble.

'You had better start on your pilgrimage at once,' said Haji Wali, meeting me the next morning with a 'goguenard' smile.

He was right. Throughout the Caravanserai nothing was talked of for nearly a week but the wickedness of the captain of Albanian Irregulars, and the hypocrisy of the staid Indian doctor. Thus it was, gentle reader, that I lost my reputation of being a 'serious person' at Cairo. And all I have to show for it is the personal experience of an Albanian drinking-bout.

I wasted but little time in taking leave of my friends, telling them, by way of precaution, that my destination was Meccah *viâ* Jeddah, and firmly determining, if possible, to make Al-Madinah *viâ* Yambu'. 'Conceal,' says the Arab's proverb, 'Thy Tenets, thy Treasure, and thy Travelling.'

Preparations to Quit Cairo

At length the slow 'month of blessings' passed away. We rejoiced like Romans finishing their Quaresima, when a salvo of artillery from the citadel announced the end of our Lenten woes. On the last day of Ramazan all gave alms to the poor, at the rate of a piastre and a half for each member of the household – slave, servant, and master. The next day, first of the three composing the Bayram or Íd (the Lesser Festival), we arose before dawn, performed our ablutions, and repaired to the Mosque, to recite the peculiar prayer of the season, and to hear the sermon which bade us be 'merry and wise.' After which we ate and drank heartily; then, with pipes and tobacco-pouches in hand, we sauntered out to enjoy the contemplation of smiling faces and street scenery.

The favourite resort on this occasion is the large cemetery beyond the Bab al-Nasr – that stern, old, massive gateway which opens upon the Suez road. There we found a scene of jollity. Tents and ambulant coffee-houses were full of men equipped in their – *anglicè* – 'Sunday best,' listening to singers and musicians, smoking, chatting, and looking at jugglers, buffoons, snake-charmers, Darwayshes, ape-leaders, and dancing boys habited in women's attire. Eating-stalls and lollipop-shops, booths full of playthings, and sheds for lemonade and syrups, lined the roads, and disputed with swings and merry-go-rounds the regards of the little Moslems and Moslemahs. The chief item of the crowd, fair Cairenes, carried in their hands huge palm branches, intending to ornament therewith the tombs of parents and friends. Yet, even on this solemn occasion, there is, they say, not a little flirtation and love-making; parties of policemen are posted, with orders to interrupt all such irregularities, with a long cane; but their vigilance is notoriously unequal to the task. I could not help observing that frequent pairs, doubtless cousins or other relations, wandered to unusual distances among the sand-hills, and that sometimes the confusion of a distant bastinado struck the ear. These trifles did not, however, by any means interfere with the general joy. Every one wore something new; most people were in the fresh suits of finery intended to last through the year; and so strong is personal vanity in the breasts of Orientals, men and women, young and old, that from Cairo to Calcutta it would be difficult to find a sad heart under a handsome coat. The men swaggered, the women minced their steps, rolled their eyes, and were eternally arranging, and coquetting with their head-veils. The little boys strutting about foully abused any one of their number who might have a richer suit than his neighbours. And the little girls ogled every one in the ecstacy of conceit, and glanced contemptuously at other little girls their rivals.

Weary of the country, the Haji and I wandered about the city, paying visits, which at this time are like

new-year calls in continental Europe. I can describe
the operation of calling in Egypt only as the discussion
of pipes and coffee in one place, and of coffee and pipes
in another. But on this occasion, whenever we meet a
friend we throw ourselves upon each other's breast,
placing right arms over left shoulders, and *vice versâ*,
squeezing like wrestlers, with intermittent hugs, then
laying cheek to cheek delicately, at the same time
making the loud noise of many kisses in the air. The
compliment of the season is, 'Kull'ám antum bil khayr'
– 'Every year may you be well!' – in fact, our 'Many
happy returns of the day!' After this come abundant
good wishes, and kindly prophecies; and from a 'religious person' a blessing, and a short prayer. To complete
the resemblance between a Moslem and a Christian
festival, we have dishes of the day, fish, Shurayk, the
cross-bun, and a peculiarly indigestible cake, called in
Egypt Kahk, the plum-pudding of Al-Islam.

This year's Íd was made gloomy, comparatively
speaking, by the state of politics. Report of war with
Russia, with France, with England, who was going to
land three million men at Suez, and with Infideldom
in general, rang through Egypt, and the city of Mars
became unusually martial. The government armouries,
arsenals, and manufactories, were crowded with kid-
napped workmen. Those who purposed a pilgrimage
feared forcible detention. Wherever men gathered
together, in the Mosques, for instance, or the coffee-
houses, the police closed the doors, and made forcible
capture of the able-bodied. This proceeding, almost as
barbarous as our impressment law, filled the main

streets with detachments of squalid-looking wretches, marching to be made soldiers, with collars round their necks and irons on their wrists. The dismal impression of the scene was deepened by crowds of women, who, habited in mourning, and scattering dust and mud over their rent garments, followed their sons, brothers, and husbands, with cries and shrieks. The death-wail is a peculiar way of cheering on the patriot departing *pro patrià mori*, and the origin of the custom is character-istic of the people. The principal public amusements allowed to Oriental women are those that come under the general name of 'Fantasia,' – birth-feasts, marriage festivals, and funerals. And the early campaigns of Mohammed Ali's family in Syria, and Al-Hijaz having, in many cases, deprived the bereaved of their sex-right to 'keen' for the dead, they have now determined not to waste the opportunity, but to revel in the luxury of woe at the live man's wake.[1]

Another cloud hung over Cairo. Rumours of con-spiracy were afloat. The Jews and Christians, – here as ready to take alarm as the English in Italy, – trembled at the fancied preparations for insurrection, massacre, and plunder. And even the Moslems whispered that some hundred desperadoes had resolved to fire the city, beginning with the bankers' quarter, and to spoil the wealthy Egyptians. Of course H. H. Abbas Pasha was absent at the time, and, even had he been at Cairo, his presence would have been of little use: the ruler can do nothing towards restoring confidence to a panic-stricken Oriental nation.

At the end of the Íd, as a counter-irritant to political

excitement, the police magistrates began to bully the people. There is a standing order in the chief cities of Egypt, that all who stir abroad after dark without a lantern shall pass the night in the station-house. But at Cairo, in certain quarters, the Azbakiyah for instance, a little laxity is usually allowed. Before I left the capital the licence was withdrawn, and the sudden strictness caused many ludicrous scenes.

If by chance you (clad in Oriental garb) had sent on your lantern to a friend's house by your servant, and had leisurely followed it five minutes after the hour of eight, you were sure to be met, stopped, collared, questioned, and captured by the patrol. You probably punched three or four of them, but found the dozen too strong for you. Held tightly by the sleeves, skirts, and collar of your wide outer garment, you were hurried away on a plane of about nine inches above the ground, your feet mostly treading the air. You were dragged along with a rapidity which scarcely permitted you to answer strings of questions concerning your name, nation, dwelling, faith, profession, and self in general, – especially concerning the present state of your purse. If you lent an ear to the voice of the charmer that began by asking a crown to release you, and gradually came down to two-pence half-penny, you fell into a simple trap; the butt-end of a musket applied *à posteriori*, immediately after the transfer of property, convicted you of wilful waste. But if, more sensibly, you pretended to have forgotten your purse, you were reviled, and dragged with increased violence of shaking to the office of the Zabit, or police magistrate. You were spun through the large archway leading to the court, every fellow in uniform giving you, as you passed, a Kafá, 'cuff,' on the back of the neck. Despite your rage, you were forced up the stairs to a long gallery full of people in a predicament like your own. Again your name, nation, – I suppose you to be masquerading, – offence, and other particulars were asked, and carefully noted in a folio by a ferocious-looking clerk. If you knew no better, you were summarily thrust into the Hásil or condemned cell, to pass the night with pick-pockets or ruffians, pell-mell. But if an adept in such matters, you insisted upon being conducted before the 'Pasha of the Night,' and, the clerk fearing to refuse, you were hurried to the great man's office, hoping for justice, and dealing out ideal vengeance to your captors, – the patrol. Here you found the dignitary sitting with pen, ink, and paper before him, and pipe and coffee-cup in hand, upon a wide Diwan of dingy chintz, in a large dimly-lit room, with two guards by his side, and a semi-circle of recent seizures vociferating before him. When your turn came, you were carefully collared, and led up to the presence, as if even at that awful moment you were mutinously and murderously disposed. The Pasha, looking at you with a vicious sneer, turned up his nose, ejaculated ''Ajami,' and prescribed the bastinado. You observed that the mere fact of being a Persian did not give mankind a right to capture, imprison, and punish you; you declared moreover that you were no Persian, but an Indian under British protection. The Pasha, a man accustomed to obedience, then stared at you, to frighten you, and you, we will suppose, stared at him, till, with an oath, he turned to the patrol, and asked them your offence. They all simultaneously swore – by Allah! – that you had been found without a lantern, dead-drunk, beating respectable people, breaking into houses, invading and robbing harims. You openly told the Pasha that they were eating abominations; upon which he directed one of his guards to smell your breath, – the charge of drunkenness being tangible. The fellow, a comrade of your capturers, advanced his nose to your lips; as might be expected, cried 'Kikh,' contorted his countenance, and answered, by the beard of 'Effendiná[2]' that he perceived a pestilent odour of distilled waters. This announcement probably elicited a grim grin from the 'Pasha of the Night,' who loves Curaçoa, and who is not indifferent to the charms of Cognac. Then by his favour, for you improved the occasion, you were allowed to spend the hours of darkness on a wooden bench, in the adjacent long gallery, together with certain little parasites, for which polite language has no name. In the morning the janissary of your Consulate was sent for: he came, and claimed you; you were led off criminally; again you gave your name and address, and if your offence was merely sending on your lantern, you were dismissed with advice to be more careful in future. And assuredly your first step was towards the Hammam.

But if, on the other hand, you had declared yourself a European, you would either have been dismissed at once, or sent to your Consul, who is here judge, jury, and jailor. Egyptian authority has of late years lost half its prestige. When Mr Lane first settled at Cairo, all Europeans accused of aggression against Moslems were, he tells us, surrendered to the Turkish magistrates. Now, the native powers have no jurisdiction over strangers, nor can the police enter their houses. If the West would raise the character of its Eastern co-religionists, it will be forced to push the system a point further, and to allow all *bonâ-fide* Christian subjects to register their names at the different Consulates whose protection they might prefer. This is what Russia has so 'unwarrantably and outrageously' attempted. We confine ourselves to a lesser injustice, which deprives Eastern states of their right as independent Powers to arrest, and to judge foreigners, who for interest or convenience settle in their dominions. But we still shudder at the right of arrogating any such claim over the born lieges of Oriental Powers. What, however, would be the result were Great Britain to authorise her sons resident at Paris, or Florence, to refuse attendance at a French or an Italian court of justice, and to demand that the police should never force the doors of an English subject? I commend this consideration to all those who 'stickle for abstract rights' when the interest and progress of others are concerned, and who become somewhat latitudinarian and concrete in cases where their own welfare and aggrandisement are at stake.

Besides patients, I made some pleasant acquaintances at Cairo. Antun Zananire, a young Syrian of considerable attainments as a linguist, paid me the compliment of permitting me to see the fair face of his

'Harím.' Mr Hatchadur Nury, an Armenian gentleman, well known in Bombay, amongst other acts of
kindness, introduced me to one of his compatriots,
Khwajah Yúsuf, whose advice was most useful to me.
The Khwajah had wandered far and wide, picking
up everywhere some scrap of strange knowledge, and
his history was a romance. Expelled from Cairo for a
youthful peccadillo, he started upon his travels, qualified himself for sanctity at Meccah and Al-Madínah,
became a religious beggar at Baghdad, studied French
at Paris, and finally settled down as a professor of
languages,[3] under an amnesty, at Cairo. In his house
I saw an Armenian marriage. The occasion was memorable: after the gloom and sameness of Moslem
society, nothing could be more gladdening than the
unveiled face of a pretty woman. Some of the guests
were undeniably charming brunettes, with the blackest
possible locks, and the brightest conceivable eyes. Only
one pretty girl wore the national costume;[4] yet they all
smoked chibuks and sat upon the Diwans, and, as they
entered the room, they kissed with a sweet simplicity
the hands of the priest, and of the other old gentlemen
present.

Among the number of my acquaintances was a
Meccan boy, Mohammed al-Basyúni, from whom I
bought the pilgrim-garb called 'Al-Ihram' and the
Kafan or shroud, with which the Moslem usually starts
upon such a journey as mine. He, being in his way
homewards after a visit to Constantinople, was most
anxious to accompany me in the character of a 'companion.' But he had travelled too much to suit me; he

had visited India, he had seen Englishmen, and he had lived with the 'Nawáb Bálú' of Surat. Moreover, he showed signs of over-wisdom. He had been a regular visitor, till I cured one of his friends of an ophthalmia, after which he gave me his address at Meccah, and was seen no more. Haji Wali described him and his party to be 'Nás jarrár' (extractors), and certainly he had not misjudged them. But the sequel will prove how *der Mensch denkt und Gott lenkt*; and as the boy, Mohammed, eventually did become my companion throughout the Pilgrimage, I will place him before the reader as summarily as possible.

He is a beardless youth, of about eighteen, chocolate-brown, with high features, and a bold profile; his bony and decided Meccan cast of face is lit up by the peculiar Egyptian eye, which seems to descend from generation to generation. His figure is short and broad, with a tendency to be obese, the result of a strong stomach and the power of sleeping at discretion. He can read a little, write his name, and is uncommonly clever at a bargain. Meccah had taught him to speak excellent Arabic, to understand the literary dialect, to be eloquent in abuse, and to be profound at Prayer and Pilgrimage. Constantinople had given him a taste for Anacreontic singing, and female society of the questionable kind, a love of strong waters, – the hypocrite looked positively scandalised when I first suggested the subject, – and an off-hand latitudinarian mode of dealing with serious subjects in general. I found him to be the youngest son of a widow, whose doting fondness had moulded his disposition; he was selfish and affectionate, as spoiled children usually are, volatile, easily offended and as easily pacified (the Oriental), coveting other men's goods, and profuse of his own (the Arab), with a matchless intrepidity of countenance (the traveller), brazen lunged, not more than half brave, exceedingly astute, with an acute sense of honour, especially where his relations were concerned (the individual). I have seen him in a fit of fury because some one cursed his father; and he and I nearly parted because on one occasion I applied to him an epithet which, etymologically considered, might be exceedingly insulting to a high-minded brother, but which in popular *parlance* signifies nothing. This '*point d'honneur*' was the boy Mohammed's strong point.

During the Ramazan I laid in my stores for the journey. These consisted of tea, coffee, loaf-sugar, rice, dates, biscuit, oil, vinegar, tobacco, lanterns, and cooking pots, a small bell-shaped tent, costing twelve shillings, and three water-skins for the Desert.[5] The provisions were placed in a 'Kafas' or hamper artistically made of palm sticks, and in a huge Sahhárah, or wooden box, about three feet each way, covered with leather or skin, and provided with a small lid fitting into the top.[6] The former, together with my green box containing medicines, and saddle-bags full of clothes, hung on one side of the camel, a counterpoise to the big Sahhárah on the other flank; the Badawin, like muleteers, always requiring a balance of weight. On the top of the load was placed transversely a Shibríyah or cot, on which Shaykh Nur squatted like a large crow. This worthy had strutted out into the streets armed with a pair of horse-pistols and a sword almost as long as himself. No sooner did the mischievous boys of Cairo – they are as bad as the *gamins* of Paris and London – catch sight of him than they began to scream with laughter at the sight of the 'Hindi (Indian) in arms,' till, like a vagrant owl pursued by a flight of larks, he ran back into the Caravanserai.

My Pilgrim Companions at Suez

I must now briefly describe the party of Meccah and Madinah men into which fate threw me: their names will so frequently appear in the following pages, that a few words about their natures will not be misplaced.

First of all comes Omar Effendi, – so called in honour, – a Dághistáni or East-Circassian, the grandson of a Hanafi Mufti at Al-Madinah, and the son of a Shaykh Rakb, an officer whose duty it is to lead dromedary-caravans. He sits upon his cot, a small, short, plump body, of yellow complexion and bilious temperament, grey-eyed, soft-featured, and utterly beardless, – which affects his feelings, – he looks fifteen, and he owns to twenty-eight. His manners are those of a student; he dresses respectably, prays regularly, hates the fair sex, like an Arab, whose affections and aversions are always in extremes; is 'serious,' has a mild demeanour, an humble gait, and a soft, slow voice. When roused he becomes furious as a Bengal tiger. His parents have urged him to marry, and he, like Kamar al-Zamán, has informed his father that he is 'a person of great age, but little sense.' Urged moreover by a melancholy turn of mind, and the want of leisure for study at Al-Madinah, he fled the paternal domicile, and entered himself a pauper Tálib 'ilm (student) in the Azhar Mosque. His disconsolate friends and afflicted relations sent a confidential man to fetch him home, by force should it be necessary; he has yielded, and is now awaiting the first opportunity of travelling gratis, if possible, to Al-Madinah.

That confidential man is a negro-servant, called Sa'ad, notorious in his native city as Al-Jinni, the Demon. Born and bred a slave in Omar Effendi's family, he obtained manumission, became a soldier in Al-Hijaz, was dissatisfied with pay perpetually in arrears, turned merchant, and wandered far and wide, to Russia, to Gibraltar, and to Baghdad. He is the pure African, noisily merry at one moment, at another silently sulky; affectionate and abusive, brave and boastful, reckless and crafty, exceedingly quarrelsome, and unscrupulous to the last degree. The bright side of his character is his love and respect for the young master, Omar Effendi; yet even him he will scold in a paroxysm of fury, and steal from him whatever he can lay his hands on. He is generous with his goods, but is ever borrowing and never paying money; he dresses like a beggar, with the dirtiest Tarbush upon his tufty poll, and only a cotton shirt over his sooty skin; whilst his two boxes are full of handsome apparel for himself and the three ladies, his wives, at Al-Madinah. He knows no fear but for those boxes. Frequently during our search for a vessel he forced himself into Ja'afar Bey's presence, and there he demeaned himself so impudently, that we expected to see him lamed by the bastinado; his forwardness, however, only amused the dignitary. He wanders all day about the bazar, talking about freight and passage, for he has resolved, cost what it will, to travel free, and, with doggedness like his, he must succeed.

Shaykh Hámid al-Sammán derives his cognomen, the 'Clarified-Butter-Seller,' from a celebrated saint and Sufi of the Kádiriyah order, who left a long line of holy descendants at Al-Madinah. This Shaykh squats upon a box full of presents for the 'daughter of his paternal uncle' (his wife), a perfect specimen of the town Arab. His poll is crowned with a rough Shúshah or tuft of hair[1]; his face is of a dirty brown, his little *goatee* straggles untrimmed; his feet are bare, and his only garment is an exceedingly unclean ochre-coloured blouse, tucked into a leathern girdle beneath it. He will not pray, because he is unwilling to take pure clothes out of his box; but he smokes when he can get other people's tobacco, and groans between the whiffs, conjugating the verb all day, for he is of active mind. He can pick out his letters, and he keeps in his bosom a little dog's-eared MS. full of serious romances and silly prayers, old and exceedingly ill written; this he will draw forth at times, peep into for a moment, devoutly kiss, and restore to its proper place with the veneration of the vulgar for a book. He can sing all manner of songs, slaughter a sheep with dexterity, deliver a grand call to prayer, shave, cook, fight; and he excels in the science of vituperation: like Sa'ad, he never performs his devotions, except when necessary to 'keep up appearances,' and though he has sworn to perish before he forgets his vow to the 'daughter of his uncle,' I shrewdly suspect he is no better than he should be. His brow crumples at the word wine, but there is quite another expression about the region of the mouth; Stambul, where he has lived some months, without learning ten words of Turkish, is a notable place for displacing prejudice. And finally, he has not more than a piastre or two in his pocket, for he has squandered the large presents given to him at Cairo and Constantinople by noble ladies, to whom he acted as master of the ceremonies at the tomb of the Apostle.

Stretched on a carpet, smoking a Persian Kaliun all day, lies Sálih Shakkar, a Turk on the father's, and an Arab on the mother's side, born at Al-Madinah. This lanky youth may be sixteen years old, but he has the ideas of forty-six; he is thoroughly greedy, selfish, and ungenerous; coldly supercilious as a Turk, and energetically avaricious as an Arab. He prays more often, and dresses more respectably, than the descendant of the Clarified-Butter-Seller; he affects the Constantinople style of toilette, and his light yellow complexion makes people consider him a 'superior person.' We were intimate enough on the road, when he borrowed from me a little money. But at Al-Madinah he cut me pitilessly, as a 'town man' does a continental acquaintance accidentally met in Hyde Park; and of course he tried, though in vain, to evade repaying his debt. He had a tincture of letters, and appeared to have studied critically the subject of 'largesse.' 'The Generous is Allah's friend, aye, though he be a Sinner, and the Miser is Allah's Foe, aye, though he be a Saint,' was a venerable saying always in his mouth. He also informed me that Pharaoh, although the quintessence of impiety, is mentioned by name in the Koran, by reason of his liberality; whereas Nimrod, another monster of iniquity, is only alluded to, because he was a stingy tyrant. It is almost needless to declare that Salih Shakkar was, as the East-Indians say, a very 'fly-sucker.²' There were two other men of Al-Madinah in the Wakalah Jirgis; but I omit description, as we left them, they being penniless, at Suez. One of them, Mohammed Shiklibhá, I afterwards met at Meccah, and seldom have I seen a more honest and warm-hearted fellow. When we were embarking at Suez, he fell upon Hamid's bosom, and both of them wept bitterly, at the prospect of parting even for a few days.

All the individuals above mentioned lost no time in opening the question of a loan. It was a lesson in Oriental metaphysics to see their condition. They had a twelve days' voyage, and a four days' journey before them; boxes to carry, custom-houses to face, and stomachs to fill; yet the whole party could scarcely, I believe, muster two dollars of ready money. Their boxes were full of valuables, arms, clothes, pipes, slippers, sweetmeats, and other 'notions'; but nothing short of starvation would have induced them to pledge the smallest article.

Foreseeing that their company would be an advantage, I hearkened favourably to the honeyed request for a few crowns. The boy Mohammed obtained six dollars; Hamid about five pounds, as I intended to make his house at Al-Madinah my home; Omar Effendi three dollars; Sa'ad the Demon two – I gave the money to him at Yambu', – and Salih Shakkar fifty piastres. But since in these lands, as a rule, no one ever lends coins, or, borrowing, ever returns them, I took care to exact service from the first, to take two rich coats from the second, a handsome pipe from the third, a 'bálá' or yataghan from the fourth, and from the fifth an imitation Cashmere shawl. After which, we sat down and drew out the agreement. It was favourable to me: I lent them Egyptian money, and bargained for repayment in the currency of Al-Hijaz, thereby gaining the exchange, which is sometimes sixteen per cent. This was done, not so much for the sake of profit, as with the view of becoming a Hátim,³ by a 'never mind' on settling day. My companions having received these small sums, became affectionate and eloquent in my praise: they asked me to make one of their number at meals for the future, overwhelmed me with questions, insisted upon a present of sweetmeats, detected in me a great man under a cloud, – perhaps my claims to being a Darwaysh assisted them to this discovery, – and declared that I should perforce be their guest at Meccah and Al-Madinah. On all occasions precedence was forced upon me; my opinion was the first con- sulted, and no project was settled without my concur- rence: briefly, Abdullah the Darwaysh suddenly found himself a person of consequence. This elevation led me into an imprudence which might have cost me dear; aroused the only suspicion about me ever expressed during the summer's tour. My friends had looked at my clothes, overhauled my medicine chest, and criti- cised my pistols; they sneered at my copper-cased watch,⁴ and remembered having seen a compass at Constantinople. Therefore I imagined they would think little about a sextant. This was a mistake. The boy Mohammed, I afterwards learned, waited only my leaving the room to declare that the would-be Haji was one of the Infidels from India, and a council sat to discuss the case. Fortunately for me, Omar Effendi had looked over a letter which I had written to Haji Wali that morning, and he had at various times received categorical replies to certain questions in high theology. He felt himself justified in declaring, *ex cathedrâ*, the boy Mohammed's position perfectly untenable. And Shaykh Hamid, who looked forward to being my host, guide, and debtor in general, and probably cared scantily for catechism or creed, swore that the light of Al-Islam was upon my countenance, and, consequently, that the boy Mohammed was a pauper, a 'fakir,' an owl, a cut-off one,[5] a stranger, and a Wahhabi (heretic), for daring to impugn the faith of a brother believer.[6] The scene ended with a general abuse of the acute youth, who was told on all sides that he had no shame, and was directed to 'fear Allah.' I was struck with the expression of my friends' countenances when they saw the sextant, and, determining with a sigh to leave it behind, I prayed five times a day for nearly a week.

We all agreed not to lose an hour in securing places on board some vessel bound for Yambu'; and my companions, hearing that my passport as a British Indian was scarcely *en règle*, earnestly advised me to have it signed by the governor without delay, whilst they occupied themselves about the harbour. They warned me that if I displayed the Turkish Tazkirah given me at the citadel of Cairo, I should infallibly be ordered to await the caravan, and lose their society and friendship. Pilgrims arriving at Alexandria, be it known to the reader, are divided into bodies, and distributed by means of passports to the three great roads, namely, Suez, Kusayr (Cosseir), and the Hajj route by land round the Gulf of al-'Akabah. After the division has once been made, government turns a deaf ear to the representations of individuals. The Bey of Suez has an order to obstruct pilgrims as much as possible till the end of the season, when they are hurried down that way, lest they should arrive at Meccah too late.[7] As most of the Egyptian high officials have boats, which sail up the Nile laden with pilgrims and return freighted with corn, the government naturally does its utmost to force the delays and discomforts of this line upon strangers.[8] And as those who travel by the Hajj route must spend money in the Egyptian territories at least fifteen days longer than they would if allowed to embark at once from Suez, the Bey very properly assists them in the former and obstructs them in the latter case. Knowing these facts, I felt that a difficulty was at hand. The first thing was to take Shaykh Nur's passport, which was *en règle*, and my own, which was not, to the Bey for signature. He turned the papers over and over, as if unable to read them, and raised false hopes high by referring me to his clerk. The under-official at once saw the irregularity of the document, asked me why it had not been visé at Cairo, swore that under such circumstances nothing would induce the Bey to let me proceed; and, when I tried persuasion, waxed insolent. I feared that it would be necessary to travel *viâ* Cosseir, for which there was scarcely time, or to transfer myself on camel-back to the harbour of Tur, and there to await the chance of finding a place in some half-filled vessel to Al-Hijaz, – which would have been relying upon an accident. My last hope at Suez was to obtain assistance from Mr West, then H.B.M.'s Vice-Consul, and since made Consul. I therefore took the boy Mohammed with me, choosing him on purpose, and excusing the step to my companions by concocting an artful fable about my having been, in Afghanistan, a benefactor to the British nation. We proceeded to the Consulate. Mr West, who had been told by imprudent Augustus Bernal to expect me, saw through the disguise, despite jargon assumed to satisfy official scruples, and nothing could be kinder than the part he took. His clerk was directed to place himself in communication with the Bey's factotum; and, when objections to signing the Alexandrian Tazkirah were offered, the Vice-Consul said that he would, at his own risk, give me a fresh passport as a British subject from Suez to Arabia. His firmness prevailed: on the second day, the documents were returned to me in a satisfactory state. I take a pleasure in owning this obligation to Mr West: in the course of my wanderings, I have often received from him open-hearted hospitality and the most friendly attentions.

The Pilgrim Ship

The larger craft anchor some three or four miles from
the Suez pier, so that it is necessary to drop down in a
skiff or shore-boat.

Immense was the confusion at the eventful hour of
our departure. Suppose us gathered upon the beach,
on the morning of a fiery July day, carefully watching
our hurriedly-packed goods and chattels, surrounded
by a mob of idlers, who are not too proud to pick
up waifs and strays; whilst pilgrims are rushing about
apparently mad; and friends are weeping, acquaintances are vociferating adieux; boatmen are demanding
fees, shopmen are claiming debts; women are shrieking
and talking with inconceivable power, and children are
crying, – in short, for an hour or so we stand in the
thick of a human storm. To confound confusion, the
boatmen have moored their skiff half a dozen yards
away from the shore, lest the porters should be unable
to make more than double their fare from the Hajis.
Again the Turkish women make a hideous noise, as
they are carried off struggling vainly in brawny arms;
the children howl because their mothers howl; and the
men scold and swear, because in such scenes none
may be silent. The moment we had embarked, each
individual found that he or she had missed something
of vital importance, – a pipe, a child, a box, or a

water-melon; and naturally all the servants were in the bazars, when they should have been in the boat. Briefly, despite the rage of the sailors, who feared being too late for a second trip, we stood for some time on the beach before putting off.

From the shore we poled to the little pier, where sat the Bey in person to perform a final examination of our passports. Several were detected without the necessary document. Some were bastinadoed, others were peremptorily ordered back to Cairo, and the rest were allowed to proceed. At about 10 A.M. (6th July) we hoisted sail, and ran down the channel leading to the roadstead. On our way we had a specimen of what we might expect from our fellow-passengers, the Maghrabi. A boat crowded with these ruffians ran alongside of us, and, before we could organise a defence, about a score of them poured into our vessel. They carried things too with a high hand, laughed at us, and seemed quite ready to fight. My Indian boy, who happened to let slip the word 'Muarras,' narrowly escaped a blow with a palm stick, which would have felled a camel. They outnumbered us, and they were armed; so that, on this occasion, we were obliged to put up with their insolence.

Our Pilgrim Ship, the Silk al-Zahab, or the 'Golden Wire,' was a Sambuk, of about 400 ardebs (fifty tons), with narrow, wedge-like bows, a clean water-line, a sharp keel, and undecked, except upon the poop, which was high enough to act as a sail in a gale of wind. She carried two masts, raking imminently forwards, the main being considerably larger than the mizzen; the former was provided with a huge triangular latine, very deep in the tack, but the second sail was unaccountably wanting. She had no means of reefing, no compass, no log, no sounding lines, no spare ropes, nor even the suspicion of a chart: in her box-like cabin and ribbed hold there was something which savoured of close connection between her model and that of the Indian Toni,[1] or 'dug-out.' Such, probably, were the craft which carried old Sesostris across the Red Sea to Deir; such were the cruisers which once every three years left Ezion-Geber for Tarshish; such the transports of which 130 were required to convey Ælius Gallus, with his 10,000 men. 'Bakhshish' was the last as well as the first odious sound I heard in Egypt. The owner of the shore-boat would not allow us to climb the sides of our vessel before paying him his fare, and when we did so, he asked for Bakhshish. If Easterns would only imitate the example of Europeans, – I never yet saw an Englishman give Bakhshish to a soul, – the nuisance would soon be done away with. But on this occasion all my companions complied with the request, and at times it is unpleasant to be singular. The first look at the interior of our vessel showed a hopeless sight; Ali Murad, the greedy owner, had promised to take sixty passengers in the hold, but had stretched the number to ninety-seven. Piles of boxes and luggage in every shape and form filled the ship from stem to stern, and a torrent of Hajis were pouring over the sides like ants into the East-Indian sugar-basin. The poop, too, where we had taken our places, was covered with goods, and a number of pilgrims had established themselves there by might, not by right.

Presently, to our satisfaction, appeared Sa'ad the Demon, equipped as an able seaman, and looking most unlike the proprietor of two large boxes full of valuable merchandise. This energetic individual instantly prepared for action. With our little party to back him, he speedily cleared the poop of intruders and their stuff by the simple process of pushing or rather throwing them off it into the pit below. We then settled down as comfortably as we could; three Syrians, a married Turk with his wife and family, the Rais or captain of the vessel, with a portion of his crew, and our seven selves, composing a total of eighteen human beings, upon a space certainly not exceeding ten feet by eight. The cabin – a miserable box about the size of the poop, and three feet high – was stuffed, like the hold of a slave ship, with fifteen wretches, children and women, and the other ninety-seven were disposed upon the luggage or squatted on the bulwarks. Having some experience in such matters, and being favoured by fortune, I found a spare bed-frame slung to the ship's side; and giving a dollar to its owner, a sailor – who flattered himself that, because it was his, he would sleep upon it, – I instantly appropriated it, preferring any hardship outside, to the condition of a packed herring inside, the place of torment.

Our Maghrabis were fine-looking animals from the deserts about Tripoli and Tunis; so savage that, but a few weeks ago, they had gazed at the cock-boat, and

wondered how long it would be growing to the size of
the ship that was to take them to Alexandria. Most of
them were sturdy young fellows, round-headed, broad-
shouldered, tall and large-limbed, with frowning eyes,
and voices in a perpetual roar. Their manners were
rude, and their faces full of fierce contempt or insolent
familiarity. A few old men were there, with countenances expressive of intense ferocity; women as savage
and full of fight as men; and handsome boys with
shrill voices, and hands always upon their daggers. The
women were mere bundles of dirty white rags. The
males were clad in 'Burnus' – brown or striped woollen
cloaks with hoods; they had neither turband nor tarbush, trusting to their thick curly hair or to the pro-
digious hardness of their scalps as a defence against the
sun; and there was not a slipper nor a shoe amongst
the party. Of course all were armed; but, fortunately
for us, none had anything more formidable than a
cut-and-thrust dagger about ten inches long. These
Maghrabis travel in hordes under a leader who obtains
the temporary title of 'Maula,' – the master. He has
generally performed a pilgrimage or two, and has collected a stock of superficial information which secures
for him the respect of his followers, and the profound
contempt of the heaven-made Ciceroni of Meccah
and Al-Madinah. No people endure greater hardships
when upon the pilgrimage than these Africans, who
trust almost entirely to alms and to other such dis-
pensations of Providence. It is not therefore to be
wondered at that they rob whenever an opportunity
presents itself. Several cases of theft occurred on board

the 'Golden Wire'; and as such plunderers seldom allow themselves to be baulked by insufficient defence, they are accused, perhaps deservedly, of having committed some revolting murders.

The first thing to be done after gaining standing-room was to fight for greater comfort; and never a Holyhead packet in the olden time showed a finer scene of pugnacity than did our pilgrim ship. A few Turks, ragged old men from Anatolia and Caramania, were mixed up with the Maghrabis, and the former began the war by contemptuously elbowing and scolding their wild neighbours. The Maghrabis, under their leader, 'Maula Ali,' a burly savage, in whom I detected a ridiculous resemblance to the Rev. Charles Delafosse, an old and well-remembered schoolmaster, retorted so willingly that in a few minutes nothing was to be seen but a confused mass of humanity, each item indiscriminately punching and pulling, scratching and biting, butting and trampling, with cries of rage, and all the accompaniments of a proper fray, whatever was obnoxious to such operations. One of our party on the poop, a Syrian, somewhat incautiously leapt down to aid his countrymen by restoring order. He sank immediately below the surface of the living mass: and when we fished him out, his forehead was cut open, half his beard had disappeared, and a fine sharp set of teeth belonging to some Maghrabi had left their mark in the calf of his leg. The enemy showed no love of fair play, and never appeared contented unless five or six of them were setting upon a single man. This made matters worse. The weaker of course drew their daggers, and a few bad wounds were soon given and received. In a few minutes five men were completely disabled, and the victors began to dread the consequences of their victory.

Then the fighting stopped, and, as many could not find places, it was agreed that a deputation should wait upon Ali Murad, the owner, to inform him of the crowded state of the vessel. After keeping us in expectation at least three hours, he appeared in a row-boat, preserving a respectful distance, and informed us that any one who pleased might quit the ship and take back his fare. This left the case exactly as it was before; none would abandon his party to go on shore: so Ali Murad rowed off towards Suez, giving us a parting injunction to be good, and not fight; to trust in Allah, and that Allah would make all things easy to us. His departure was the signal for a second fray, which in its accidents differed a little from the first. During the previous disturbance we kept our places with weapons in our hands. This time we were summoned by the Maghrabis to relieve their difficulties, by taking about half a dozen of them on the poop. Sa'ad the Demon at once rose with an oath, and threw amongst us a bundle of 'Nabbút' – goodly ashen staves six feet long, thick as a man's wrist, well greased, and tried in many a rough bout. He shouted to us 'Defend yourselves if you don't wish to be the meat of the Maghrabis!' and to the enemy – 'Dogs and sons of dogs! now shall you see what the children of the Arab are.' 'I am Omar of Daghistan!' 'I am Abdullah the son of Joseph!' 'I am Sa'ad the Demon!' we exclaimed, 'renowning it' by this display of name and patronymic. To do our enemies justice, they showed no sign of flinching; they swarmed towards the poop like angry hornets, and encouraged each other with cries of 'Allaho akbar!' But we had a vantage-ground about four feet above them, and their palm-sticks and short daggers could do nothing against our terrible quarter-staves. In vain the 'Jacquerie,' tried to scale the poop and to overpower us by numbers; their courage only secured them more broken heads.

At first I began to lay on load with *main morte*, really fearing to kill some one with such a weapon; but it soon became evident that the Maghrabis' heads and shoulders could bear and did require the utmost exertion of strength. Presently a thought struck me. A large earthen jar full of drinking water,[2] – in its heavy frame of wood the weight might have been 100 lbs., – stood upon the edge of the poop, and the thick of the fray took place beneath. Seeing an opportunity, I crept up to the jar, and, without attracting attention, rolled it down by a smart push with the shoulder upon the swarm of assailants. The fall caused a shriller shriek to rise above the ordinary din, for heads, limbs, and bodies were sorely bruised by the weight, scratched by the broken potsherds, and wetted by the sudden discharge. A fear that something worse might be coming made the Maghrabis slink off towards the end of the vessel. After a few minutes, we, sitting in grave silence, received a deputation of individuals in whity-brown Burnus, spotted and striped with what Mephistopheles calls a 'curious juice.' They solicited peace, which we granted upon the condition that they would pledge themselves to keep it. Our heads, shoulders, and hands were penitentially kissed, and presently the fellows returned to bind up their hurts in dirty rags. We owed this victory entirely to our own exertions, and the meek Omar was by far the fiercest of the party. Our Rais, as we afterwards learned, was an old fool who could do nothing but call for the Fátihah, claim Bakhshish at every place where we moored for the night, and spend his leisure hours in the 'Caccia del Mediterraneo.' Our crew consisted of half a dozen Egyptian lads, who, not being able to defend themselves, were periodically chastised by the Maghrabis, especially when any attempt was made to cook, to fetch water, or to prepare a pipe.

At length, about 3 P.M. on the 6th July, 1853, we shook out the sail, and, as it bellied in the favourable wind, we recited the Fatihah with upraised hands which we afterwards drew down our faces. As the 'Golden Wire' started from her place, I could not help casting one wistful look upon the British flag floating over the Consulate. But the momentary regret was stifled by the heart-bounding which prospects of an adventure excite, and by the real pleasure of leaving Egypt. I had lived there a stranger in the land, and a hapless life it had been: in the streets every man's face, as he looked upon the Persian, was the face of a foe. Whenever I came in contact with the native officials, insolence marked the event; and the circumstance of living within hail of my fellow-countrymen, and yet finding it impossible to enjoy their society, still throws a gloom over the memory of my first sojourn in Egypt.

The ships of the Red Sea – infamous region of rocks, reefs, and shoals – cruise along the coast by day, and at night lay-to in the first cove they find; they do not sail when it blows hard, and as in winter time the weather is often stormy and the light of day does not last long, the voyage is intolerably slow. At sunset we stayed our adventurous course; and, still within sight of Suez, comfortably anchored under the lee of Jabal Atakah, the 'Mountain of Deliverance,' the butt-end of Jabal Joshí. We were now on classic waters. The Eastern shore was dotted with the little grove of palm-trees which clusters around the Uyun Musa, or Moses' Wells; and on the west, between two towering ridges, lay the mouth of the valley (Bádiyah, or Wady Tawarik, or Wady Musa) down which, according to Father Sicard, the Israelites fled to the Sea of Sedge. The view was by no means deficient in a sort of barbarous splendour. Verdure there was none, but under the violet and orange tints of the sky the chalky rocks became heaps of topazes, and the brown-burnt ridges masses of amethyst. The rising mists, here silvery white, there deeply rosy, and the bright blue of the waves, lining long strips of golden sand, compensated for the want of softness by a semblance of savage gorgeousness.

Next morning (7th July), before the cerulean hue had vanished from the hills, we set sail. It was not long before we came to a proper sense of our position. The box containing my store of provisions, and, worse still, my opium, was at the bottom of the hold, perfectly unapproachable; we had, therefore, the pleasure of breaking our fast on 'Mare's skin,'[3] and a species of biscuit, hard as a stone and quite as tasteless. During the day, whilst insufferable splendour reigned above, the dashing of the waters below kept my nest in a state of perpetual drench. At night rose a cold, bright moon, with dews falling so thick and clammy that the skin felt as though it would never be dry again. It is, also, by no means pleasant to sleep upon a broken cot about four feet long by two broad, with the certainty that a false movement would throw you overboard, and a conviction that if you do fall from a Sambuk under sail, no mortal power can save you. And as under all circumstances in the East, dozing is one's chief occupation, the reader will understand that the want of it left me in utter, utter idleness.

The gale was light that day, and the sunbeams were fire; our crew preferred crouching in the shade of the sail to taking advantage of what wind there was. In spite of our impatience we made but little way: near evening time we anchored on a tongue of sand, about two miles distant from the well-known and picturesque heights called by the Arabs Hammam Faraún,[4] which

> –'like giants stand
> To sentinel enchanted land.'

The strip of coarse quartz and sandstone gravel is obviously the offspring of some mountain torrent; it stretches southwards, being probably disposed in that direction by the currents of the sea as they receive the deposit. The distance of the 'Hammam Bluffs' prevented my visiting them, which circumstance I regretted the less as they have been described by pens equal to the task.

That evening we enjoyed ourselves upon clean sand, whose surface, drifted by the wind into small yellow waves, was easily converted by a little digging and heaping up, into the coolest and most comfortable of couches. Indeed, after the canescent heat of the day, and the tossing of our ill-conditioned vessel, we should have been contented with lodgings far less luxurious. Fuel was readily collected, and while some bathed, others erected a hearth – three large stones and a hole open to leeward – lit the fire and put the pot on to boil. Shaykh Nur had fortunately a line; we had been successful in fishing; a little rice also had been bought; with this boiled, and rock-cod broiled upon the charcoal, we made a dinner that caused every one to forget the sore grievance of 'Mare's skin' and stone-hard biscuit. A few Maghrabis had ventured on shore, the Rais having terrified the others by threatening them with those 'bogies,' the Badawin – and they offered us Kuskusu[5] in exchange for fish.

At Yambu'

The heat of the sun, the heavy dews, and the frequent washings of the waves, had so affected my foot, that on landing at Yambu' I could scarcely place it upon the ground. But traveller's duty was to be done; so, leaning upon my 'slave's' shoulder, I started at once to see the town, whilst Shaykh Hamid and the others of our party proceeded to the custom-house.

Yanbu'a al-Bahr, Yambu' or Fountain of the Sea, identified, by Abyssinian Bruce, with the Iambia village of Ptolemy, is a place of considerable importance, and shares with others the title of 'Gate of the Holy City.' It is the third quarter of the caravan road[1] from Cairo to Meccah; and here, as well as at Al-Badr, pilgrims frequently leave behind them, in hired warehouses, goods too heavy to be transported in haste, or too valuable to risk in dangerous times. Yambu' being the port of Al-Madinah, as Jeddah is of Meccah, is supported by a considerable transport trade and extensive imports from the harbours on the Western coasts of the Red Sea; it supplies its chief town with grain, dates, and henna. Here the Sultan's dominion is supposed to begin, whilst the authority of the Pasha of Egypt ceases; there is no Nizám, or Regular Army, however, in the town,[2] and the governor is a Sharíf or Arab chief. I met him in the great bazar; he is a fine young man of

light complexion and the usual high profile, hand-
somely dressed, with a Cashmere turband, armed to
the extent of sword and dagger, and followed by
two large, fierce-looking Negro slaves leaning upon
enormous Nabbuts.

The town itself is in no wise remarkable. Built on
the edge of a sunburnt plain that extends between the
mountains and the sea, it fronts the northern extremity
of a narrow winding creek. Viewed from the harbour,
it is a long line of buildings, whose painful whiteness
is set off by a sky-like cobalt and a sea-like indigo;
behind it lies the flat, here of a bistre-brown, there of
a lively tawny; whilst the background is formed by
dismal Radhwah,

'Barren and bare, unsightly, unadorned.'

Outside the walls are a few little domes and tombs,
which by no means merit attention. Inside, the streets
are wide; and each habitation is placed at an unsociable
distance from its neighbour, except near the port and
the bazars, where ground is valuable. The houses are
roughly built of limestone and coralline, and their walls
full of fossils crumble like almond cake; they have huge
hanging windows, and look mean after those in the
Moslem quarters of Cairo. There is a 'Suk,' or market-
street of the usual form, a long narrow lane darkened
by a covering of palm leaves, with little shops let into
the walls of the houses on both sides. The cafés, which
abound here, have already been described in the last
chapter; they are rendered dirty in the extreme by

travellers, and it is impossible to sit in them without a fan to drive away the flies. The custom-house fronts the landing-place upon the harbour; it is managed by Turkish officials, – men dressed in Tarbushes, who repose the live-long day upon the Diwans near the windows. In the case of us travellers they had a very simple way of doing business, charging each person of the party three piastres for each large box, but by no means troubling themselves to meddle with the contents. Yambu' also boasts of a Hammam or hot bath, a mere date-leaf shed, tenanted by an old Turk, who, with his surly Albanian assistant, lives by 'cleaning' pilgrims and travellers. Some whitewashed Mosques and Minarets of exceedingly simple form, a Wakalah or two for the reception of merchants, and a saint's tomb, complete the list of public buildings.

In one point Yambu' claims superiority over most other towns in this part of Al-Hijaz. Those who can afford the luxury drink sweet rain-water, collected amongst the hills in tanks and cisterns, and brought on camel-back to the town. Two sources are especially praised, the Ayn al-Birkat and the Ayn Ali, which suffice to supply the whole population: the brackish water of the wells is confined to coarser purposes. Some of the old people here, as at Suez, are said to prefer the drink to which years of habit have accustomed them, and it is a standing joke that, arrived at Cairo, they salt the water of the Nile to make it palatable.

The population of Yambu' – one of the most bigoted and quarrelsome races in Al-Hijaz – strikes the eye after arriving from Egypt, as decidedly a new feature.

The Shaykh or gentleman is over-armed and over-dressed, as Fashion, the Tyrant of the Desert as well as of the Court, dictates to a person of his consequence. The civilised traveller from Al-Madinah sticks in his waistshawl a loaded pistol, garnished with crimson silk cord, but he partially conceals the butt-end under the flap of his jacket. The Irregular soldier struts down the street a small armoury of weapons: one look at the man's countenance suffices to tell you what he is. Here and there stalk grim Badawin, wild as their native wastes, and in all the dignity of pride and dirt; they also are armed to the teeth, and even the presence of the policeman's quarterstaff cannot keep their swords in their scabbards. What we should call the peaceful part of the population never leave the house without the 'Nabbut' over the right shoulder, and the larger, the longer, and the heavier the weapon is, the more gallantry does the bearer claim. The people of Yambu' practise the use of this implement diligently; they become expert in delivering a head-blow so violent as to break through any guard, and with it they always decide their trivial quarrels. The dress of the women differs but little from that of the Egyptians, except in the face veil, which is generally white. There is an independent bearing about the Yambu' men, strange in the East; they are proud without insolence, and they look manly without blustering. Their walk partakes somewhat of the nature of a swagger, owing, perhaps, to the shape of the sandals, not a little assisted by the self-esteem of the wearer, but there is nothing offensive in it: moreover, the population has a healthy appearance, and, fresh from Egypt, I could not help noticing their freedom from ophthalmic disease. The children, too, appear vigorous, nor are they here kept in that state of filth to which fear of the Evil Eye devotes them in the Valley of the Nile.

Hijazi Dress

I must now take the liberty of presenting to the reader an Arab Shaykh fully equipped for travelling. Nothing can be more picturesque than the costume, and it is with regret that we see it exchanged in the towns and more civilised parts for any other. The long locks or the shaven scalps are surmounted by a white cotton skull-cap, over which is a Kúfíyah – a large square kerchief of silk and cotton mixed, and generally of a dull red colour with a bright yellow border, from which depend crimson silk twists ending in little tassels that reach the wearer's waist. Doubled into a triangle, and bound with an *Aakal* or fillet of rope, a skein of yarn or a twist of wool, the kerchief fits the head close behind: it projects over the forehead, shading the eyes, and giving a fierce look to the countenance. On certain occasions one end is brought round the lower part of the face, and is fastened behind the head. This veiling the features is technically called *Lisâm*: the chiefs generally fight so, and it is the usual disguise when a man fears the avenger of blood, or a woman starts to take her *Sar*. In hot weather it is supposed to keep the Samun, in cold weather the catarrh, from the lungs.

The body dress is simply a *Kamís* or cotton shirt: tight sleeved, opening in front, and adorned round the waist and collar, and down the breast, with embroidery like net-work; it extends from neck to foot. Some wear wide trousers, but the Badawin consider such things effeminate, and they have not yet fallen into the folly of socks and stockings. Over the Kamís is thrown a long-skirted and short-sleeved cloak of camel's hair, called an Abá. It is made in many patterns, and of all materials from pure silk to coarse sheep's wool; some prefer it brown, others white, others striped: in Al-Hijaz the favourite hue is white, embroidered with gold,[1] tinsel, or yellow thread in two large triangles, capped with broad bands and other figures running down the shoulders and sides of the back. It is lined inside the shoulders and breast with handsome stuffs of silk and cotton mixed, and is tied in front by elaborate strings, and tassels or acorns of silk and gold. A sash confines the Kamís at the waist, and supports the silver-hilted *Jambíyah*[2] or crooked dagger: the picturesque Arab sandal[3] completes the costume. Finally, the Shaykh's arms are a sword and a matchlock slung behind his back; in his right hand he carries a short javelin or a light crooked stick, about two feet and a half long, called a *Mas'hab*, used for guiding camels.

The poorer clans of Arabs twist round their waist, next to the skin, a long plait of greasy leather, to support the back; and they gird the shirt at the middle merely with a cord, or with a coarse sash. The dagger is stuck in this scarf, and a bandoleer slung over the shoulders carries the cartridge-case, powder-flask, flint and steel, priming-horn, and other necessaries. With the traveller, the waist is an elaborate affair. Next to the skin is worn the money-pouch, concealed by the

Kamís; the latter is girt with a waist shawl, over which is strapped a leathern belt. The latter article should always be well garnished with a pair of long-barrelled and silver-mounted flint pistols,[4] a large and a small dagger, and an iron ramrod with pincers inside; a little leathern pouch fastened to the waist-strap on the right side contains cartridge, wadding, and flask of priming powder. The sword hangs over the shoulder by crimson silk cords and huge tassels[5]: well-dressed men apply the same showy ornaments to their pistols. In the hand may be borne a bell-mouthed blunderbuss; or, better still, a long single-barrel gun with an ounce bore. All these weapons must shine like silver, if you wish to be respected; for the knightly care of arms is here a sign of manliness.

Pilgrims, especially those from Turkey, carry, I have said, a 'Hamail,' to denote their holy errand. This is a pocket Koran, in a handsome gold-embroidered crimson velvet or red morocco case, slung by red silk cords over the left shoulder. It must hang down by the right side, and should never depend below the waist-belt. For this I substituted a most useful article. To all appearance a 'Hamail,' it had inside three compartments; one for my watch and compass, the second for ready money, and the third contained penknife, pencils, and slips of paper, which I could hold concealed in the hollow of my hand. These were for writing and drawing: opportunities of making a 'fair copy' into the diary-book,[6] are never wanting to the acute traveller. He must, however, beware of sketching before the Badawin, who would certainly proceed to extreme measures, suspecting him to be a spy or a sorcerer.[7] Nothing so effectually puzzles these people as the Frankish habit of putting everything on paper; their imaginations are set at work, and then the worst may be expected from them. The only safe way of writing in presence of a Badawi would be when drawing out a horoscope or preparing a charm; he also objects not, if you can warm his heart upon the subject, to seeing you take notes in a book of genealogies. You might begin with, 'And you, men of Harb, on what origin do you pride yourselves?' And while the listeners became fluent upon the, to them, all-interesting theme, you could put down whatever you please upon the margin. The townspeople are more liberal, and years ago the Holy Shrines have been drawn, surveyed and even lithographed, by Eastern artists: still, if you wish to avoid all suspicion, you must rarely be seen with pen or with pencil in hand.

Arriving in Sight of Al-Madinah

The sun had nearly risen (July 25th) before I shook off
the lethargic effects of such a night. All around me
were hurrying their camels, regardless of rough ground,
and not a soul spoke a word to his neighbour. 'Are
there robbers in sight?' was the natural question. 'No!'
replied Mohammed; 'they are walking with their eyes,
they will presently see their homes!' Rapidly we passed
the Wady al-Akik, of which,

'O my friend, this is Akik, then stand by it,
Endeavouring to be distracted by love, if not really a lover,'

and a thousand other such pretty things, have been
said by the Arab poets. It was as 'dry as summer's
dust,' and its 'beautiful trees' appeared in the shape of
vegetable mummies. Half an hour after leaving the
'Blessed Valley' we came to a huge flight of steps
roughly cut in a long broad line of black scoriaceous
basalt. This is termed the Mudarraj or flight of steps
over the western ridge of the so-called Al-Harratayn.
It is holy ground; for the Apostle spoke well of it.
Arrived at the top, we passed through a lane of dark
lava, with steep banks on both sides, and after a few
minutes a full view of the city suddenly opened upon us.
    We halted our beasts as if by word of command. All

of us descended, in imitation of the pious of old, and sat down, jaded and hungry as we were, to feast our eyes with a view of the Holy City.

'O Allah! this is the Harim (sanctuary) of Thy Apostle; make it to us a Protection from Hell Fire, and a Refuge from Eternal Punishment! O open the Gates of Thy Mercy, and let us pass through them to the Land of Joy!' and 'O Allah, bless the last of Prophets, the Seal of Prophecy, with Blessings in number as the Stars of Heaven, and the Waves of the Sea, and the Sands of the Waste – bless him, O Lord of Might and Majesty, as long as the Corn-field and the Date-grove continue to feed Mankind!' And again, 'Live for ever, O Most Excellent of Prophets! – live in the Shadow of Happiness during the Hours of Night and the Times of Day, whilst the Bird of the Tamarisk (the dove) moaneth like the childless Mother, whilst the West-wind bloweth gently over the Hills of Nijd, and the Lightning flasheth bright in the Firmament of Al-Hijaz!'

Such were the poetical exclamations that rose all around me, showing how deeply tinged with imagination becomes the language of the Arab under the influence of strong passion or religious enthusiasm. I now understood the full value of a phrase in the Moslem ritual, 'And when his' (the pilgrim's) 'eyes shall *fall upon the Trees of Al-Madinah,* let him raise his Voice and bless the Apostle with the choicest of Blessings.' In all the fair view before us nothing was more striking, after the desolation through which we had passed, than the gardens and orchards about the town. It was impossible not to enter into the spirit of my companions, and truly I believe that for some minutes my enthusiasm rose as high as theirs. But presently when we remounted, the traveller returned strong upon me: I made a rough sketch of the town, put questions about the principal buildings, and in fact collected materials for the next chapter.

Notes

To Alexandria

1. 'Then came Trafalgar: would that Nelson had known the meaning of that name! it would have fixed a smile upon his dying lips!' so says the Rider through the Nubian Desert, giving us in a foot note the curious information that 'Trafalgar' is an Arabic word, which means the '*Cape of Laurels*.' Trafalgar is nothing but a corruption of Tarf al-Ghárb – the side or skirt of the West; it being the most occidental point then reached by Arab conquest.

2. 'Praise be to Allah, Lord of the (three) worlds!' a pious ejaculation, which leaves the lips of the True Believer on all occasions of concluding actions.

3. In a coarser sense 'kayf' is applied to all manner of intoxication. Sonnini is not wrong when he says, 'the Arabs give the name of Kayf to the voluptuous relaxation, the delicious stupor, produced by the smoking of hemp.'

4. A Persian as opposed to an Arab.

5. A priest, elder, chieftain, language-master, private-tutor, &c., &c.

6. The Mandal is that form of Oriental divination which owes its present celebrity in Europe to Mr Lane. Both it and the magic mirror are hackneyed subjects, but I have been tempted to a few words concerning them in another part of these volumes. Meanwhile I request the reader not to set me down as a mere charlatan; medicine

in the East is so essentially united with superstitious practices, that he who would pass for an expert practitioner, must necessarily represent himself an 'adept.'

7. The Persian 'Mister.' In future chapters the reader will see the uncomfortable consequences of my having appeared in Egypt as a Persian. Although I found out the mistake, and worked hard to correct it, the bad name stuck to me; bazar reports fly quicker and hit harder than newspaper paragraphs.

8. Arab Christians sometimes take the name of 'Abdullah,' servant of Allah – 'which,' as a modern traveller observes, 'all sects and religions might be equally proud to adopt.' The Moslem Prophet said, 'the names most approved of God are Abdullah, Abd-al-rahman (Slave of the Compassionate), and such like.'

9. 'King in-the-name-of-Allah,' a kind of Oriental 'Praise-God-Barebones.' When a man appears as a Fakir or Darwaysh, he casts off, in process of regeneration, together with other worldly sloughs, his laical name for some brilliant coat of nomenclature rich in religious promise.

10. A Murshid is one allowed to admit Murids or apprentices into the order.

11. The Taríkat or path, which leads, or is supposed to lead, to Heaven.

Restlessness

1. The long pipe which at home takes the place of the shorter chibúk used on the road.

Planning for the Journey

1. A stick of soft wood chewed at one end. It is generally used throughout the East, where brushes should be avoided, as the natives always suspect hogs' bristles.
2. Almost all Easterns sleep under a sheet, which becomes a kind of respirator, defending them from the dews and mosquitoes by night and the flies by day. The 'rough and ready' traveller will learn to follow the example, remembering that 'Nature is founder of Customs in savage countries;' whereas, amongst the *soi-disant* civilised, Nature has no deadlier enemy than Custom.
3. It is strictly forbidden to carry arms in Egypt. This, however, does not prevent their being as necessary – especially in places like Alexandria, where Greek and Italian ruffians abound – as they ever were in Rome or Leghorn during the glorious times of Italian 'liberty.'
4. In the Azhar Mosque, immediately after Friday service, a fellow once put his hand into my pocket, which fact alone is ample evidence of 'progress.'
5. As a general rule, always produce, when travelling, the minutest bit of coin. At present, however, small change is dear in Egypt; the Sarráfs, or money-changers, create the dearth in order to claim a high agio. The traveller must prepare himself for a most unpleasant task in learning the different varieties of currency, which appear all but endless, the result of deficiency in the national circulating medium. There are, however, few copper coins, the pieces of ten or five faddah (or parahs), whereas silver and gold abound. As regards the latter metal, strangers should mistrust all small pieces, Turkish as well as Egyptian. 'The greater part are either cut

or cracked, or perhaps both, and worn down to mere spangles: after taking them, it will not be possible to pass them without considerable loss.' Above all things, the traveller must be careful never to change gold except in large towns, where such a display of wealth would not arouse suspicion or cupidity; and on no occasion when travelling even to pronounce the ill-omened word 'Kís' (purse). Many have lost their lives by neglecting these simple precautions.

6. Some prefer a long chain of pure gold divided into links and covered with leather, so as to resemble the twisted girdle which the Arab fastens round his waist. It is a precaution well known to the wandering knights of old. Others, again, in very critical situations, open with a lancet the shoulder, or any other fleshy part of the body, and insert a precious stone, which does not show in its novel purse.

On the Nile Steamboat the 'Little Asthmatic'

1. Those skilled in simples, Eastern as well as Western, praise garlic highly, declaring that it 'strengthens the body, prepares the constitution for fatigue, brightens the sight, and, by increasing the digestive power, obviates the ill-effects arising from sudden change of air and water.' The traveller inserts it into his dietary in some pleasant form, as 'Provence-butter,' because he observes that, wherever fever and ague abound, the people, ignorant of cause but observant of effect, make it a common article of food. The old Egyptians highly esteemed this vegetable, which, with onions and leeks, enters into the list of articles so much regretted by the Hebrews

(Numbers, xi. 5; Koran, chap. 2). The modern people of the Nile, like the Spaniards, delight in onions, which, as they contain between 25 and 30 per cent. of gluten, are highly nutritive. In Arabia, however, the stranger must use this vegetable sparingly. The city people despise it as the food of a Fellah – a boor. The Wahhabis have a prejudice against onions, leeks, and garlic, because the Prophet disliked their strong smell, and all strict Moslems refuse to eat them immediately before visiting the mosque, or meeting for public prayer.

2. A policeman.

Life in the Wakálah

1. This familiar abbreviation of Wali al-Dín was the name assumed by the enterprising traveller, Dr Wallin.

2. By the Indians called Bhang, the Persians Bang, the Hottentots Dakhá, and the natives of Barbary Fasúkh. Even the Siberians, we are told, intoxicate themselves by the vapour of this seed thrown upon red-hot stones. Egypt surpasses all other nations in the variety of compounds into which this fascinating drug enters, and will one day probably supply the Western world with 'Indian hemp,' when its solid merits are duly appreciated. At present in Europe it is chiefly confined, as cognac and opium used to be, to the apothecary's shelves. Some adventurous individuals at Paris, after the perusal of Monte Christo, attempted an 'orgie' in one of the cafés, but with poor success.

3. The Indian name of an Afghan, supposed to be a corruption of the Arabic Fat'hán (a conqueror), or a derivation from the Hindustani *paithna*, to penetrate (into

the hostile ranks). It is an honourable term in Arabia, where 'Khurásani' (a native of Khorasan), leads men to suspect a Persian, and the other generic appellation of the Afghan tribes 'Sulaymáni,' a descendant from Solomon, reminds the people of their proverb, 'Sulaymáni hárámi!' – 'the Afghans are ruffians!'

The Cost of Living in Cairo

1. There are four kinds of tobacco smoked in Egypt. The first and best is the well-known Latakia, generally called 'Jabali,' either from a small seaport town about three hours' journey south of Latakia, or more probably because grown on the hills near the ancient Laodicea. Pure, it is known by its blackish colour, fine shredding, absence of stalk, and an undescribable odour, to me resembling that of creosote; the leaf, too, is small, so that when made into cigars it must be covered over with a slip of the yellow Turkish tobacco called Báfrá. Except at the highest houses unadulterated Latakia is not to be had in Cairo. Yet, mixed as it is, no other growth exceeds it in flavour and fragrance. Miss Martineau smoked it, we are told, without inconvenience, and it differs from our Shag, Bird's-eye, and Returns, in degree, as does Château Margeau from a bottle of cheap strong Spanish wine. To bring out its flavour, the connoisseur smokes it in long pipes of cherry, jasmine, maple, or rosewood, and these require a servant skilled in the arts of cleaning and filling them. The best Jabali at Cairo costs about seven piastres the pound; after which a small sum must be paid to the Farram or chopper, who prepares it for use.

2nd. Súri (Tyrian), or Shámi, or Suryáni, grown in Syria, an inferior growth, of a lighter colour than Latakia, and with a greenish tinge; when cut, its value is about three piastres per pound. Some smokers mix this leaf with Jabali, which, to my taste, spoils the flavour of the latter without improving the former. The strongest kind, called Koráni or Jabayl, is generally used for cigarettes; it costs, when of first-rate quality, about five piastres per pound.

3rd. Tumbak, or Persian tobacco, called Hijazi, because imported from the Hijaz, where everybody smokes it, and supposed to come from Shíráz, Kázerún, and other celebrated places in Persia. It is all but impossible to buy this article unadulterated, except from the caravans returning after the pilgrimage. The Egyptians mix it with native growths, which ruins its flavour and gives it an acridity that 'catches the throat,' whereas good tumbak never yet made a man cough. Yet the taste of this tobacco, even when second-rate, is so fascinating to some smokers that they will use no other. To be used it should be wetted and squeezed, and it is invariably inhaled through water into the lungs: almost every town has its favourite description of pipe, and these are of all kinds, from the pauper's rough cocoa-nut mounted with two reeds, to the prince's golden bowl set with the finest stones. Tumbak is cheap, costing about four piastres a pound, but large quantities of it are used.

4th. Hummi, as the word signifies, a 'hot' variety of the tumbak, grown in Al-Yaman and other countries. It is placed in the tile on the búri or cocoa-nut pipe, unwetted, and has a very acrid flavour. Being supposed to produce intoxication, or rather a swimming in the head, hummi gives its votaries a bad name: respectable men would answer 'no' with rage if asked whether they are smoking it, and when a fellow tells you that he has seen better days, but that now he smokes Hummi in a buri, you understand him that his misfortunes have affected either his brain or his morality. Hence it is that this tobacco is never put into pipes intended for smoking the other kinds. The price of Hummi is about five piastres per pound.

The Ramazan

1. Of course all quarrelling, abuse, and evil words are strictly forbidden to the Moslem during Ramazan. If one believer insult another, the latter should repeat 'I am fasting' three times before venturing himself to reply. Such is the wise law. But human nature in Egypt, as elsewhere, is always ready to sacrifice the spirit to the letter, rigidly to obey the physical part of an ordinance, and to cast away the moral, as if it were the husk and not the kernel.
2. 'Allah opens' (the door of daily bread) is a polite way of informing a man that you and he are not likely to do business; in other words, that you are not in want of his money.
3. The summons to prayer.
4. One of our wants is a history of the bell and its succedanai. Strict Moslems have an aversion to all modifications of this instrument, striking clocks, gongs, &c., because they were considered by the Prophet peculiar to the devotions of Christians. He, therefore, instituted the Azan, or call to prayer, and his followers still clap their hands when we should ring for a servant. The symbolical meaning of the bell, as shown in the sistrum

of Isis, seems to be the movement and mixture of the elements, which is denoted by clattering noise. 'Hence,' observes a learned antiquary, 'the ringing of bells and clattering of plates of metal were used in all lustrations, sacrifices, &c.' We find them amongst the Jews, worn by the high priest; the Greeks attached them to images of Priapus, and the Buddhists of Thibet still use them in their worship, as do the Catholics of Rome when elevating the Host.

5. Al-Ghada is the early dinner: Al-Asha, the supper, eaten shortly after sunset.

6. Extra prayers repeated in the month of Ramazan. They take about an hour, consisting of 23 prostrations, with the Salam (or blessing on the Prophet) after every second prostration.

7. Strangers often wonder to see a kind of cemetery let into a dwelling-house in a crowded street. The reason is, that some obstinate saint has insisted upon being buried there, by the simple process of weighing so heavily in his bier, that the bearers have been obliged to place him on the pavement. Of course, no good Moslem would object to have his ground floor occupied by the corpse of a holy man. The reader will not forget, that in Europe statues have the whims which dead bodies exhibit in Egypt. So, according to the Abbé Marche, the little statue of Our Lady, lately found in the forest of Pennacom, 'became, notwithstanding her small size, heavy as a mountain, and would not consent to be removed by any one but the chaplain of the chateau.'

8. A daughter, a girl. In Egypt, every woman expects to be addressed as 'O lady!' 'O female-pilgrim!' 'O bride!' or, 'O daughter!' even though she be on the wrong side of fifty. In Syria and in Arabia, you may say 'y'al mara!'

(O woman); but if you attempt it near the Nile, the answer of the offended fair one will be 'may Allah cut out thy heart!' or, 'the *woman*, please Allah, in thine eye!' And if you want a violent quarrel, 'y'al agúz!' (O old woman!) pronounced drawlingly, – y'al ago-o-ooz, – is sure to satisfy you. On the plains of Sorrento, in my day, it was always customary, when speaking to a peasant girl, to call her 'bella fé,' (beautiful woman), whilst the worst of insults was 'vecchiarella.' So the Spanish Calesero, under the most trying circumstances, calls his mule 'Vieja, rivieja,' (old, very old). Age, it appears, is as unpopular in Southern Europe as in Egypt.

The Albanian Captain

1. The stiff, white, plaited kilt worn by Albanians.
2. Vulgarly Rákí, the cognac of Egypt and Turkey. Generically the word means any spirit; specifically, it is applied to that extracted from dates, or dried grapes. The latter is more expensive than the former, and costs from 5 to 7 piastres the bottle. It whitens the water like Eau de Cologne, and being considered a stomachic, is patronised by Europeans as much as by Asiatics. In the Azbakiyah gardens at Cairo, the traveller is astonished by perpetual 'shouts' for 'Sciroppo di gomma,' as if all the Western population was afflicted with sore throat. The reason is that spirituous liquors in a Moslem land must not be sold in places of public resort; so the infidel asks for a 'syrup of gum,' and obtains a 'dram' of 'Araki. The favourite way of drinking it, is to swallow it neat, and to wash it down with a mouthful of cold water. Taken in this way it acts like the 'petit verre d'absinthe.'

Egyptian women delight in it, and Eastern topers of all classes and sexes prefer it to brandy and cognac, the smell of which, being strange, is offensive to them.

3. The 'Salatah' is made as follows. Take a cucumber, pare, slice and place it in a plate, sprinkling it over with salt. After a few minutes, season it abundantly with pepper, and put it in a bowl containing some peppercorns, and about a pint of curds. When the dish is properly mixed, a live coal is placed upon the top of the compound to make it bind, as the Arabs say. It is considered a cooling dish, and is esteemed by the abstemious, as well as by the toper.

4. These Albanians are at most half Asiatic as regards manner. In the East generally, the host drinks of the cup, and dips his hand into the dish before his guest, for the same reason that the master of the house precedes his visitor over the threshold. Both actions denote that no treachery is intended, and to reverse them, as amongst us, would be a gross breach of custom, likely to excite the liveliest suspicions.

5. Formerly these places, like the coffee-houses, were crowded with bad characters. Of late years the latter have been refused admittance, but it would be as easy to bar the door to gnats and flies. They appear as 'foot-pages,' as washerwomen, as beggars; in fact, they evade the law with ingenuity and impunity.

6. *Anglicè*, Alexandria, Cairo, and Suez, – an extensive field of operations.

Preparations to Quit Cairo

1. 'There were no weeping women; no neighbours came in to sit down in the ashes, as they might have done had the soldier died at home; there was no Nubian dance for the dead, no Egyptian song of the women lauding the memory of the deceased, and beseeching him to tell why he had left them alone in the world to weep.' – (Letter from Widdin, March 25, 1854, describing a Turkish soldier's funeral.)

2. 'Our lord,' i.e. H. H. the Pasha. 'Kikh' is an interjection nothing disapproval, or disgust, – 'Fie!' or 'Ugh!'

3. Most Eastern nations, owing to their fine ear for sounds, are quick at picking up languages; but the Armenian is here, what the Russian is in the West, the *facile princeps* of conversational linguists. I have frequently heard them speak with the purest accent, and admirable phraseology, besides their mother tongue, Turkish, Arabic, Persian, and Hindustani, nor do they evince less aptitude for acquiring the Occidental languages.

4. It has been too frequently treated of, to leave room for a fresh description. Though pretty and picturesque, it is open to the reproach of Moslem dressing, namely, that the in-door toilette admits of a display of bust, and is generally so scanty and flimsy that it is unfit to meet the eye of a stranger. This, probably the effect of secluding women, has now become a cause for concealing them.

5. Almost all the articles of food were so far useful, that they served every one of the party at least as much as they did their owner. My friends drank my coffee, smoked my tobacco, and ate my rice. I bought better tea at Meccah than at Cairo, and found as good sugar

there. It would have been wiser to lay in a small stock merely for the voyage to Yambu', in which case there might have been more economy. But I followed the advice of those interested in setting me wrong. Turks and Egyptians always go pilgrimaging with a large outfit, as notably as the East-Indian cadet of the present day, and your outfitter at Cairo, as well as Cornhill, is sure to supply you with a variety of superfluities. The tent was useful to me; so were the water-skins, which I preferred to barrels, as being more portable, and less liable to leak. Good skins cost about a dollar each; they should be bought new and always kept half full of water.

6. This shape secures the lid, which otherwise, on account of the weight of the box, would infallibly be torn off, or burst open. Like the Kafas, the Sahhárah should be well padlocked, and if the owner be a saving man, he does not entrust his keys to a servant. I gave away my Kafas at Yambu', because it had been crushed during the sea-voyage, and I was obliged to leave the Sahhárah at Al-Madinah, as my Badawi camel-shaykh positively refused to carry it to Meccah, so that both these articles were well nigh useless to me. The Kafas cost four shillings, and the Sahhárah about twelve. When these large boxes are really strong and good, they are worth about a pound sterling each.

My Pilgrim Companions at Suez

1. When travelling, the Shushah is allowed to spread over the greatest portion of the scalp, to act as a protection against the sun; and the hair being shaved off about two inches all round the head, leaves a large circular patch.

Nothing can be uglier than such tonsure, and it is contrary to the strict law of the Apostle, who ordered a clean shave, or a general growth of the hair. The Arab, however, knows by experience, that though habitual exposure of the scalp to a burning sun may harden the skull, it seldom fails to damage its precious contents. He, therefore, wears a Shushah during his wanderings, and removes it on his return home. Abu Hanifah, if I am rightly informed, wrote a treatise advocating the growth of a long lock of hair on the Násiyah, or crown of the head, lest the decapitated Moslem's mouth or beard be exposed to defilement by an impure hand. This would justify the comparing it to the 'chivalry-lock,' by which the American brave facilitates the removal of his own scalp. But I am at a loss to discover the origin of our old idea, that the 'angel of death will, on the last day, bear all true believers, by this important tuft of hair on the crown, to Paradise.' Probably this office has been attributed to the Shushah by the ignorance of the West.

2. 'Makhí-chús,' equivalent to our 'skin-flint.'
3. A well-known Arab chieftain, whose name has come to stand for generosity itself.
4. This being an indispensable instrument for measuring distances, I had it divested of gold case, and provided with a facing carefully stained and figured with Arabic numerals. In countries where few can judge of a watch by its works, it is as well to secure its safety by making the exterior look as mean as possible. The watches worn by respectable people in Al-Hijaz are almost always old silver pieces, of the turnip shape, with hunting cases and an outer *étui* of thick leather. Mostly they are of Swiss or German manufacture, and they find their way into Arabia *viâ* Constantinople and Cairo.

5. Munkati'a – one cut off (from the pleasures and comforts of life). In Al-Hijaz, as in England, any allusion to poverty is highly offensive.
6. The Koran expressly forbids a Moslem to discredit the word of any man who professes his belief in the Saving Faith. The greatest offence of the Wahhabis is their habit of designating all Moslems that belong to any but their own sect by the opprobrious name of Kafirs or infidels. This, however, is only the Koranic precept; in practice a much less trustful spirit prevails.
7. Towards the end of the season, poor pilgrims are forwarded gratis, by order of government. But, to make such liberality as inexpensive as possible, the Pasha compels ship-owners to carry one pilgrim per 9 ardebs (about 5 bushels each), in small, and 1 per 11 in large vessels.
8. I was informed by a Prussian gentleman, holding an official appointment under His Highness the Pasha, at Cairo, that 300,000 ardebs of grain were annually exported from Kusayr to Jeddah. The rest is brought down the Nile for consumption in Lower Egypt, and export to Europe.

The Pilgrim Ship

1. The Toni or Indian canoe is the hollowed-out trunk of a tree, – near Bombay generally a mango. It must have been the first step in advance from that simplest form of naval architecture, the 'Catamaran' of Madras and Aden.
2. In these vessels each traveller, unless a previous bargain be made, is expected to provide his own water and firewood. The best way, however, is, when the old

wooden box called a tank is sound, to pay the captain
for providing water, and to keep the key.

3. Jild al-Faras (or Kamar al-Din), a composition of apricot
paste, dried, spread out, and folded into sheets, exactly
resembling the article after which it is named. Turks
and Arabs use it when travelling; they dissolve it in
water, and eat it as a relish with bread or biscuit.

4. 'Pharaoh's hot baths,' which in our maps are called
'Hummum Bluffs.' They are truly 'enchanted land' in
Moslem fable: a volume would scarcely contain the
legends that have been told and written about them.

5. One of the numerous species of what the Italians generally call 'Pasta.' The material is wheaten or barley flour
rolled into small round grains. In Barbary it is cooked
by steaming, and served up with hard boiled eggs and
mutton, sprinkled with red pepper. These Badawi
Maghrabis merely boiled it.

At Yambu'

1. The first quarter of the Cairo caravan is Al-Akabah;
the second is the Manhal Salmah (Salmah's place for
watering camels); the third is Yambu'; and the fourth
Meccah.

2. The Nizam, as Europeans now know, is the regular
Turkish infantry. In Al-Hijaz, these troops are not sta-
tioned in small towns like Yambu'. At such places a
party of Irregular horse, for the purpose of escorting
travellers, is deemed sufficient. The Yambu' police
seems to consist of the Sharif's sturdy negroes. In Ali
Bey's time Yambu' belonged to the Sharif of Meccah,
and was garrisoned by him.

Hijazi Dress

1. Gold, however, as well as silk, I may be excused for re-peating, is a forbidden article of ornament to the Moslem.

2. The silver-hilted dagger is a sign of dignity: 'I would silver my dagger,' in idiomatic Hijazi, means, 'I would raise myself in the world.'

3. Niebuhr has accurately described this article. It is still worn in the Madras army, though long discarded from the other presidencies; the main difference between the Indian and the Arab sandal is, that the former has a ring, into which the big toe is inserted, and the latter a thong, which is clasped between the big toe and its neighbour. Both of them are equally uncomfortable, and equally injurious to soldiers, whose legs fight as much as do their arms. They abrade the skin wherever the straps touch, expose the feet to the sun, wind, and rain, and admit thorns and flints to the toes and toe-nails. In Arabia, the traveller may wear, if he pleases, slippers, but they are considered townsman-like and effeminate. They must be of the usual colours, red or yellow. Black shoes, though almost universally worn by the Turks at Cairo and Constantinople, would most probably excite suspicion in Al-Hijaz.

4. It is as well to have a good pair of Turkish barrels and stocks, fitted up with locks of European manufacture; those made by natives of these countries can never be depended upon. The same will apply to the gun or rifle. Upon the whole, it is more prudent to have flint locks. Copper caps are now sold in the bazars of Meccah and Al-Madinah, where a Colt's 'six-shooter' might excite attention for a day; but were the owner in a position to

despise notoriety, he might display it everywhere without danger. One of our guards, who was killed on the road, had a double-barrelled English fowling-piece. Still, when doubts must not be aroused, the traveller will do well to avoid, even in the civilised Hijaz, suspicious appearances in his weapons. I carried in a secret pocket a small pistol with a spring dagger, upon which dependence could be placed, and I was careful never to show it, discharging it and loading it always in the dark. Some men wear a little dagger strapped round the leg, below the knee. Its use is this: when the enemy gets you under, he can prevent you bringing your hand up to the weapon in your waist-belt; but before he cuts your throat, you may slip your fingers down to the knee, and persuade him to stop by a stab in the perineum. This knee dagger is required only in very dangerous places. The article I chiefly accused myself of forgetting was a stout English clasp-knife, with a large handle, a blade like an 'Arkansas toothpick,' and possessing the other useful appliances of picker, fleam, tweezers, lancet, and punch.

5. Called 'Habak': these cords are made in great quantities at Cairo, which possesses a special bazar for them, and are exported to all the neighbouring countries, where their price considerably increases. A handsome pistol-cord, with its tassels, costs about 12 shillings in Egypt; at Meccah, or Al-Madinah, the same would fetch upwards of a pound sterling.

6. My diary-book was made up for me by a Cairene; it was a long thin volume fitting into a breast-pocket, where it could be carried without being seen. I began by writing notes in the Arabic character, but as no risk appeared, my journal was afterwards kept in English. More than once, by way of experiment, I showed the

writing on a loose slip of paper to my companions, and astonished them with the strange character derived from Solomon and Alexander, the Lord of the Two Horns, which we Afghans still use. For a short trip a pencil suffices; on long journeys ink is necessary; the latter article should be English, not Eastern, which is washed out clean the first time your luggage is thoroughly soaked with rain. The traveller may use either the Persian or the brass Egyptian ink-stand; the latter, however, is preferable, being stronger and less likely to break. But, unless he be capable of writing and reading a letter correctly, it would be unadvisable to stick such an article in the waist-belt, as this gives out publicly that he is a scribe. When sketching, the pencil is the best, because the simplest and shortest mode of operation is required. Important lines should afterwards be marked with ink, as 'fixing' is impossible on such journeys. For prudence sake, when my sketches were made, I cut up the paper into square pieces, numbered them for future reference, and hid them in the tin canisters that contained my medicines.

7. An accident of this kind happened not long ago, in Hazramaut, to a German traveller who shall be nameless. He had the mortification to see his sketch-book, the labour of months, summarily appropriated and destroyed by the Arabs. I was told by a Hazramaut man at Cairo, and by several at Aden, that the gentleman had at the time a narrow escape with his life; the Badawín wished to put him to death as a spy, sent by the Frank to *ensorceler* their country, but the Shaykhs forbade bloodshed, and merely deported the offender. Travellers caught sketching are not often treated with such forbearance.